THE ART & BUSINESS OF CREATIVE
SELF-PROMOTION

FOR GRAPHIC DESIGNERS, WRITERS, ILLUSTRATORS & PHOTOGRAPHERS

THE ART & BUSINESS OF CREATIVE
SELF-PROMOTION

FOR GRAPHIC DESIGNERS, WRITERS, ILLUSTRATORS & PHOTOGRAPHERS

JERRY HERRING & MARK FULTON

WATSON-GUPTILL PUBLICATIONS/NEW YORK

Copyright © 1987 by Watson-Guptill Publications

First published 1987 in New York by Watson-Guptill Publications,
a division of Billboard Publications, Inc.,
1515 Broadway, New York, New York 10036

Library of Congress Cataloging-in-Publication Data

Herring, Jerry.
 The art & business of creative self-promotion.
 1. Graphic arts—Marketing. 2. Sales promotion.
I. Fulton, Mark. II. Title. III. Title: Art and
business of creative self-promotion.
NC1001.H47 1987   741.6′068′8   87-13360
ISBN 0-8230-0248-9

First published in Great Britain in 1987 by
Columbus Books, Ltd., 19-23 Ludgate Hill
London EC4M 7PD
ISBN 0-86287-390-8

Produced by Jerry and Sandy Herring, Graphic Design Press
Designed by Jerry Herring
Design and production assistance by Tom McNeff
Typography by Characters, Inc.

Manufactured in Japan

3 4 5 6 7 8 9 10/92 91 90

CONTENTS

PREFACE

In the title of our book we say, "The Art & Business of Creative Self-Promotion." Maybe we should say something about the art *versus* the business. With creative people, the art often gets in the way of the business. For lots of reasons (some of them temperamental, some having to do with the way we were trained) many of us take a perverse pride in being non-business people. Or pretending to be. Our excuse is that we're creative. We brag about never missing a deadline, and then laugh about how long it takes us to get around to filling out our timesheets or doing our billing. And we believe that our best way of getting business is to sit by the phone and wait.

There's something we should remember. Our creativity can bring us two things. Money and fun. But usually if we aren't making any money, creativity isn't much fun. On the other hand, San Francisco designer Michael Vanderbyl says, "I will do any job, no matter what amount of money the client has, if it is something that, in the end, will be fun and will help me to move into another market."

Another San Francisco designer has a warning for us when it comes to fun. Primo Angeli says, "We never talk about 'fun.' You have to realize what you're communicating to your client when you say 'fun.' For him this is serious business. There's a lot at stake. *You're* having 'fun?' *He's* working his tail off. He doesn't want to hear about 'fun.' He wants to know that what you're doing for him is going to *work*."

Both of these comments come from the kinds of creative people we most admire—the ones who are the most inventive, the ones who get the most respect, the ones who make the most money, and probably have the most fun—and who are usually the best business people too. These are the people who have been able to create their own special business environments or those who can perform successfully in the business environments of agencies or studios. So let's get down to business. The business of self-promotion.

INTRODUCTION

THE WHYS

To get exactly the kind of work you want is the best reason for *why* you should do self-promotion. Strange as it may seem, if no one has ever heard of you, or seen your work, you are starting out with an advantage. Perceived image is the key here. If people have seen only one kind of work from you, they'll assume that's *all* you do. For example, let's suppose you're a photographer with a full-service studio, but location shots are all anybody sees of your work. Location shots are what they'll call you for. Your self-promotion can change that perception. Or create an image.

Of course, you may be getting exactly the kind of work you want to do. This can be a trap as well. No client relationship lasts forever, so it is important that while you are producing your present assignments, you are planning for your future projects as well. If you are not expanding your contacts, you are most certainly losing ground to your competitors.

Another part of the "I already have the kind of work that I want" trap is, surprisingly, you may get too much of it. Too much of a good thing? Yes, it happens to creative people every day. Once you are known for a certain type of work, a certain style, a certain field of expertise, you may have so much to do within this certain area that you don't have the time or inclination to expand your work or your client base. Then, if the style changes, or the particular business segment becomes depressed, you are not in a position to move on to other fields, other projects.

The answer to *why* you should produce self-promotion is exposure. You need to let more people know what you are doing or want to do, and you can do that with self-promotion. But just *what* is self-promotion?

LIST #1
WHAT DO I WANT MY SELF-PROMOTION TO ACCOMPLISH?

• Establish/develop image
• Change perceived image
• Position talent in market place
• Get more work
• Get different kind of work
• Get better work
• Get better-paying work
• Expand client base
• Relocate geographically

Be positive, specific. Keep this list in mind while you plan your self-promotion.

THE WHATS

Self-promotion is something (or anything) you do for yourself that:
> *–establishes, changes, or enhances your image,*
> *–positions you in the creative marketplace, and/or*
> *–develops new business contacts for you.*

What you do is limited only by your imagination, talent, ingenuity, and, to a lesser extent, your budget.

The first and most important thing you have to do is this: Define exactly what you want to accomplish with your self-promotion. Is it more work? Better work? Better-paying work? Different work? A location change? Recognition and respect from your peers? Awards? Whatever it is, make a list. Seriously, sit down and write out a list.

You also need to think about what form your promotion will take: a brochure, a poster, an ad, a postcard, a collection of your best work, a calendar, a party, or what? The medium pretty much depends upon what you want to accomplish, who you are and/or what you want to be, your experience, and what you're doing now. You should be able to define your objectives and resources easily, but most people don't give it much thought. Colin Forbes of Pentagram (London/New York/San Francisco) does. As he says, "I sit down first thing each morning and remind myself what business I'm in." We would add to that, *"and what business I want to be in."*

Obviously, what you do for your self-promotion does depend upon what business you're in.

> *–Designers should design.*
> *–Copywriters should write.*
> *–Photographers should photograph.*
> *–And illustrators should illustrate.*

And if you're a designer who needs copy, photography, or illustration to make your design work, don't try to do it yourself unless you're as good a writer, photographer, or illustrator as you are a designer. Get the best you can find. The same thing goes for a writer, photographer, or illustrator who needs design, and so on. We'll talk more about creative teams for self-promotion when we get to the Hows. But first let's think about just *when* to promote yourself.

THE WHENS

If you haven't started your self-promotion project yet, you're already behind. The perfect axiom for self-promotion comes from Houston designer Jack Amuny: "If you're busy, you won't do it; if you're not busy, it's too late." All *you* have to do is become an exception to that rule.

One of the major disciplines that needs to be mastered to produce good self-initiated projects is to become as critical of these projects as you are with client projects. Most often, the client provides the necessary parameters that make our projects work: budget, schedule, and judgment. The client determines a project's appropriateness, seeing the big picture (the entire business) while we are concerned with the details (the project). When producing promotional materials, this necessary outside force is missing, forcing these reponsibilities on us. So no matter how busy you are, *schedule* your promotion project. Right now. Treat it like a regular, paying job. And stick to your schedule. Even if it interferes with a project with a quicker payoff. In the long run you'll be glad you did.

Take advantage of the moment. It is amazing how important timing is. Don't underestimate such clichés as "Strike while the iron is hot" or "Make hay while the sun shines." When you have just gone out on your own or had an anniversary or won an award or moved or whatever, it is time to take advantage of the moment. It is noteworthy then and only then. It is a reason to make contact.

And making contact is what self-promotion is all about. It is the process of making people aware that you are out there, that you want their business, and that you will be able to do it if you get it. So many times a buying decision is made on the spur of the moment, and it is at these times that you want your name to come to mind. (We have been told by art directors, when asked why they used a particular photographer, that the photographer's mailer had just come across their desk at the time they were making a decision about who to use.) For large projects, a list may be drawn up of prospective creative suppliers. You want clients to think of you when the list is being drawn up. Whether you receive the work may depend on talent, cost, personality, and availability; however, you cannot compete in an arena that you are not in.

That brings up another point. When should you expect your self-promotion to pay off? We have to say that it depends upon the Whys and Whats of your project: why you're doing it and what you expect it to accomplish. We've seen first-time/one-time promotion pieces strongly focused to elicit from new clients a terrific response. But usually it's a more gradual, building process. The greater your expectations, the longer it'll usually take to achieve them. In any case, those great self-promotion ideas in your notebook and those tissue layouts in your drawer aren't going to accomplish anything, now or later, if you don't get moving. But even if nothing's happening (maybe especially if nothing's happening) *now* is when to start. All you need to do now is figure out *how*.

THE HOWS

Make your second list now: your audience or prospect list. Look at the list of goals you just made. Then list the people who can help you accomplish those goals. Start with the general categories of people, like agency creative directors, corporate communications managers, and so on. Then list individual companies, and, finally, write down names of specific people. If you don't know the names, phone the agencies or companies and ask. You'll find most receptionists happy to cooperate, especially if you don't want to *talk* to the person in question. Just mention that you're putting something in the mail and need the right name.

Think about the broad categories of the potential marketplaces for your talents. Then make your promotion fit those needs. Do you want to do advertising? Print or broadcast? Are you interested in corporate communications? Annual reports or marketing-support collateral? What about publishing? Magazines or books?

WHO SHOULD I DIRECT MY
SELF–PROMOTION TOWARD?

Define your broad audience
• Advertising agencies
• Design firms
• Public relations firms
• Public companies
• Specific corporate or service
  categories (doctors, clothing
  manufacturers, computer
  companies, etc.)
• Colleges
• Foundations
• Publishers
• Others

Then, refine the list to titles

• Creative director
• Account executive
• Art director
• Writer/producer
• Corporate communications
  director
• Director of financial relations
• Marketing manager
• Information services director
• Editor
• Photo editor
• Others

Once you have defined your market,
make your list by specific name,
title, address and phone number.
After you have established a list, you
will need to constantly update as
people are promoted or move, and
with new prospects you develop.

A recent survey indicated that there are *twice as many buyers of creative talent as there are sellers.* For example, in advertising agencies billing $1 million or more, there are close to 20,000 creative directors, art directors, copywriters, producers, production managers, and others who are buyers of outside creative services. Add to this the corporate, publishing, and retail communities and the actual total number of buyers for your work is mind boggling. What you have to do is locate the individuals right for you, do something to impress them, and keep on impressing them.

Once you've got your prospect list, you can start thinking about the promotion itself. And here's a critical point: *What you do must be of some value to your prospects*—preferably of *great* value. Ideally he or she should want to keep your piece forever. Or at least get enough out of it to remember it, and you. That's tougher than it sounds. Most self-promotion pieces go *directly* into the trash. Even some of the really good stuff gets this treatment. So you need your promotion to seem to be too valuable to discard.

How do we define value? *Value is having your prospects think of you as a resource.* Just like you, your prospects also have things that they want to accomplish professionally. You want them to see you as someone who can help them get what *they* want. You want them to see that you're exactly the designer, the writer, the photographer, or the illustrator they need.

Ideally, the individual pieces of your self-promotion should look like the kind of work you want to get. If you want to do brochures, do a brochure. If you want to do annual reports, your piece should be compatible with the annual report field. If you want to do broadcast creative, do a demo tape—either audio or video. If you want to do ads, do an ad. And with an ad, you really don't have to place it in a publication. You can send it out as a "reprint" (or actually as a "preprint"). Of course if it makes sense to run it somewhere, and you can afford it, run it—in The Creative Black Book© or an American Showcase annuals, for example. (More about the annual directories on pages 130-135.)

Sometimes all you have to do is show how good you are. Maybe all you need is a collection of your best work shown in a brochure, a tape, an ad, or whatever. But usually it takes something more. The noise level is pretty high out there. You might need to do more than display your work. Here's where your imagination comes into play, and where you might need some help. This brings us to the creative-team approach.

We, as creative individuals, interface daily with other creative disciplines and technical suppliers. We need to use these resources to promote our clients. Luckily for us, many of these individuals and firms need promoting as well, which gives the opportunity for the "promotional partnership." This is hardly a new concept. People have been scratching each other's backs in every conceivable business, in every conceivable way, for as long as anyone would want to remember. However, it is important to keep in mind that for a promotional partnership to work, it must be good for both parties. So when you ask the printer, or writer or designer or whomever to come to your aid, be aware of how the project can benefit *that* individual or firm as well as your own. How can the project be a benefit, as opposed to a burden? We are often reminded that there is no "free lunch." So don't expect one.

Many creative teams are made up of just two talents, such as a writer and a designer, or a designer and a photographer. These people may work together on a project that mutually promotes both talents. After the project is printed, both parties distribute the piece to promote themselves, and at the same time expose the other partner to new potential clients.

Be open about who you might approach to become involved in your project. Designers, writers, photographers, illustrators, typesetters, printers and color separators are the obvious first group. Keep in mind retouchers, editors, reps, PR consultants, video producers, and photo labs.

A more complicated, yet more financially attractive, form of creative partnership is the combination of creative individuals with technical suppliers. A creative person (or persons) creates a poster or brochure or whatever and then asks a typesetter and printer to contribute their services for credit and exposure. The piece must adequately display the work of the suppliers, and you may be required to show off a technique or service that they want to promote (a new typeface, for example, or a varnishing technique). Other times, the suppliers may just want to be associated with high quality work. This indicates that the best suppliers to approach may be those that have the ability to produce the quality you require, but may not be the biggest or the highest profile suppliers in town. These partnerships can help everyone involved because all have something that the other needs: creatives generally cannot afford the cost of reproducing their work, and suppliers may not be able to afford the cost of good quality design, writing, photography, or illustration.

It is probably a good idea to insert here that "trade outs," that is trading your services for someone else's services, can have tax implications that may vary from state to state. Consult your accountant before you make any assumptions.

There are also opportunities for exposure where you are producing the kind of work you want to—for real clients. Nonprofit organizations provide such opportunities for you to promote yourself while helping them promote themselves. It's a case of "if they look good, you look good." Most charitable organizations have a great need for promotional material and no budget. What this means to the creative volunteer is creative freedom. The Creative Control Rule applies here: *"If they want to pay a lot of money, they can have a lot of control. If they want to pay a little bit of money, they can have a little bit of control. And if they don't want to pay anything, they can stand and watch."* But keep in mind that the object first and foremost is to communicate your clients' needs. Another benefit is that you meet other volunteers who can be valuable contacts for regular business.

Art directors clubs, photographers organizations, and similar creative groups also have need for promotional material and also allow considerable creative freedom. Usually there's considerable competition for this work, and you should keep in mind that with all this creative freedom, you've got no excuse for doing less than terrific work.

One of the more obvious ways to promote your skills is through the many local and national awards competitions that are conducted annually. Success in these competitions can help promote your career within the profession. They may be the single most influential force that helps staff people at agencies and studios as well as corporations and in-house groups become recognized and move up the ladder within their organizations. Employers use the published annuals to recruit creative talent. And many buyers of creative services use the awards annuals as reference for freelance talent.

Success in awards competitions can help with clients, as well. Clients like awards. And award winners. And they like their work to win awards. At the end of a project it is nice for your client to be able to show his or her superiors that the work they have been buying has brought positive recognition.

Last but not least is the positive effect award shows can have on your own self-confidence. It is important to know that you are doing good work, and that others think so too.

So enter. But pick the competitions that can best promote you and your clients. (See pages 138-141 for a list of creative competitions.) The most important forums are going to be; 1) your local competitions; 2) shows that are published so that they are accessible; and 3) shows that may be of special interest to your client, such as an annual report competition or restaurant menu competition. Shows to stay away from are those that are outside of your market and will have little impact for your business. There are many, many shows, and you can spend a small fortune paying entry and hanging fees. So it is important to have a plan of which competitions are best for you to enter, and stick to it.

BE A JOINER

Up to now we've talked mostly about the more visible, visual aspects of creative self-promotion. But there are some other ways to promote yourself. To begin with, you should *become a joiner.* Join professional organizations. Join community associations. Join hobby groups. Get out there and talk to people, people with common interests or goals. These contacts can be an invaluable source for new business and referrals.

While you're at it, it's also a good idea to take a course or two in public speaking. You can usually find them in your local adult education program. Community colleges offer speech classes that will also help you immensely. You can also join the Toastmasters for additional practice—and more contacts. You'll find yourself more relaxed in the board room at annual report time and even in one-on-one conversations with clients and associates. You'll be able to accept speaking engagements that will be coming your way as a recognized creative professional. You'll have fun, too.

FOLLOW-UP

Mailing out a sensational promotional piece may not be enough. You may need to follow up. The form of self-promotion that most creative people find extremely difficult to do is the cold call. We just don't seem to be comfortable calling on someone we don't know. It's especially hard with someone who might never have heard of us. But for the right person, cold calls can be very effective. Los Angeles designer Ken White does a lot of print media self-promotion, *and* he makes cold calls, "...*all* the time. Sometimes I'll phone maybe twenty people in one day, and go see six or so. I'll do that for two or three days in a row." It works for him, even though he adds, "It can *really* be a humbling experience." What you want to achieve with the follow-up call is an interview. This is what all the promotion is aimed at.

As for the interview itself, probably the best advice we can give is *don't talk too much.* You don't have to explain each and every piece of your work. Let your prospective clients or employers set the pace. Ask them about their business. Show them that you're interested in more than just the project or the job. Be friendly, but not forward. And be yourself. A day or so after the interview, send a brief note thanking the people involved for their time and reiterating your interest. Several photographers that we know send a photo print along with the note. This is a nice touch—especially if the prospect happened to remark about a particular shot.

BECOME A JOINER

Join the professional organizations that you qualify for, both national and local. There are professional clubs and organizations for every creative discipline (many of which are listed on pages 142-143 of this book). Become an active member, volunteer, and work on committees. Then think about expanding your contacts beyond the professional circles, to organizations such as:

• Chambers of Commerce
• Breakfast clubs
• Church groups
• Social or sports clubs
• Nonprofit volunteer groups
• Arts groups
• Discussion groups
• Continuing education classes

Another form of promotion you may consider is outside professional help. Professional representatives, or "reps," are most commonly used by photographers and illustrators, but some designers and writers are using them now, too. Reps do just what the title implies, they represent you to potential clients. They do pretty much what agents do for entertainment people.

The great thing about having a rep is that you can be working at what you do best and making money (and enjoying your work) while your rep is out there getting more work for you to do. With a rep (or reps) you can have a presence in a city (or cities) away from where you live or work. They generally work on a percentage of the revenue of the work they bring in (15, 20, or 25 percent, depending on your reputation and ability to attract work). But they often are able to negotiate a better deal than you could. And if you're good, a good rep will keep you busy.

Scott Hull, a national artist representative working out of Ohio, adds: "I would say that a good rep educates his illustrator or photographer to be a better business manager, making him or her aware of pricing, contract negotiations, and rights. Of course, the main thing that a rep can do is present the work to new markets. The rep has the time to devote to clients one on one, which is a real advantage for the talent. I want to devote my time to their careers to help them grow and become successful, and as they do I'll be getting a percentage of their profits which will be earned because my efforts helped *them* to develop."

Another outside professional you should consider is the public relations consultant. A PR person or firm can get your name out to the public (read: prospects) in a way that you just can't do yourself. They are good for more than just publicity. That's part of it, of course, but a good PR person will get involved with your *entire* marketing program—including your self-promotion. They will work to make you more visible. This means that your prospects will feel more secure about you because they *know* about you. A PR consultant can gain exposure for you in media that you may not know how to approach, such as local newspapers and magazines, and the growing number of business publications. Says Houston marketing consultant Larry Taylor, "I can do things that you can't because I am a disinterested third party. I can call up the features or business editor and say, 'You really need to do a feature on this person. She is really doing exciting work.' It's okay for me to say that. It's not okay for you to."

How you pick your PR outfit depends upon how you work. If you're a freelancer, pick a freelance consultant, who will understand your problems and your budget. If you have a staff of thirty people, go for a PR firm of about the same size, and so on.

THE ARTIST REPRESENTATIVE

WHAT CAN A REP DO FOR YOU?

- Expand contracts
- Upgrade income level
- Provide more time to create
- Provide wider exposure (regional, national)

WHAT DOES A REP LOOK FOR?

- Someone whose work the rep can sell to his or her market (local, regional or national)
- Someone whose work is unique
- Someone who is professional, consistent, and dependable
- Someone whose work will be compatible with the other work the rep currently represents

WHAT DOES A REP COST?

Reps work on a percentage of work brought in, anywhere from 15% to 30%, based on reputation and ability to attract work. Initially, you will need to spend money to prepare your portfolio for presentation, and you will need to help pay for promotional materials. (Most reps will pay the same percentage as their commission, for example, a rep charging 25% commission would pay 25% of the cost for ads or mailers.)

WHAT IS REQUIRED?

You will need to sign a contract with the rep, and give him or her an exclusive right to an area. You may have more than one rep, if their territories do not overlap.

The most overlooked form of self-promotion is promoting yourself with the clients you already have. We often forget that it is easier to keep clients we have than to attract new ones. Yet we will spend more time and money wooing prospective clients than we will spend to make sure that the ones we have know how much they are appreciated. Assuming that you are doing a good job for your clients, and they like what you are doing, go the extra step and thank them.

Give gifts that are inexpensive but mean something to the client. This is very important, because the last thing you want to do is insult clients by appearing to buy their favor or make them feel indebted to you. What you want is for them to feel good about working with you. A nice bottle of wine might be appropriate, or some flowers. Books are always good. By now, you know the people well enough to know what their tastes and interests are. Use sound judgment—and don't overspend.

Be attentive. Show your interest in the business. If you read something in a magazine or newspaper that applies, send a clipping with a short note. Send candid photos taken during a project. Use your imagination. Keep your clients or supervisors thinking about you in a positive way. *Don't ever take them for granted.*

As we've said before, the toughest thing about self-promotion is getting started. The things we say about creative self-promotion in this book should be a help to you in organizing your own promotion. We're pretty sure you'll find the examples we've picked to be inspirational.

Always remember that self-promotion, whatever the form, is a building process. Keep at it. It'll pay off. It has for all the people represented in this book.

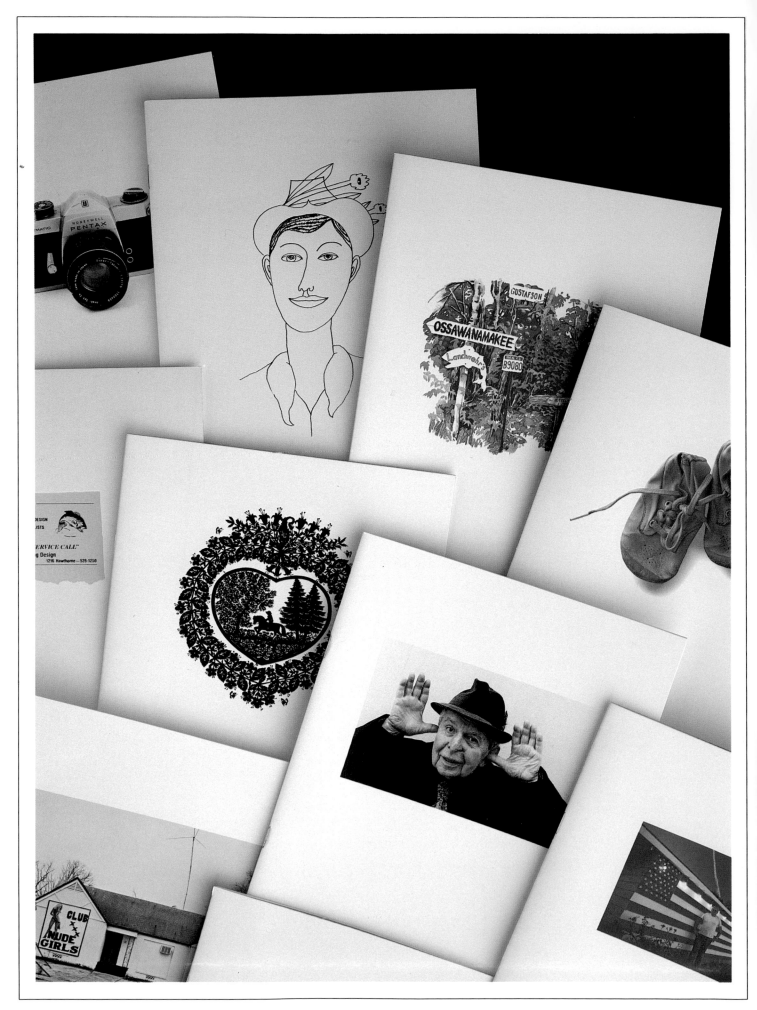

Herring Design, founded in 1973, has established a reputation over the years that has been enhanced by the constant stream of self-promotion materials the firm has produced. Starting when the firm was made up of Jerry Herring and two pieces of furniture.

You might say that I've made a career out of self-promotion. Or even that self-promotion has made my career.

For me, self-promotion has meant a series of different approaches. Early on, I was trying to create an identity for myself in the ad and design business and at the same time influence employers. As I began my own business, the goal was to establish an image among agency art directors, my first real business base. And finally, as my business expanded to include corporations and institutions, the focus of the self-promotion efforts changed again.

While I was with Stan Richards & Associates in Dallas, two of the studio's projects became very influential in my thinking about promotion. The first was an assignment from Stan to design a business card for a local photographer, Moses Olmos. Stan often rejected the expected approach, and his direction to me was to work the configuration of Moses' name, such as the never-ending: MOSESOLMOSESOL MOSESOLMOSESOLMOSES. My eventual solution was a card that slid back and forth inside a folded sleeve. To me, the importance of this piece was that it promoted a photographer, not with photographs, but with a play on letters. The solution was one that could only apply to Moses, and, when handed to a prospective client, would create interest and a reason to retain the card. It also appealed to the special sensitivities of an art director or a designer. This became a valuable lesson in the importance of image, and the value of a unique solution.

The second influential piece at Stan Richards was a booklet designed and illustrated by Jim Jacobs. It was called *Hobo Signs*, and was produced as a joint promotional piece for Stan Richards & Associates and a printer, Canterbury Press.

This was my first look at a cooperative effort, one that was designed to be helpful to both parties. The studio was able to have a promotional mailout, yet did not have to pay for the most expensive part of the project, the printing. The printer benefitted from a valuable marketing tool, one that was well designed and produced by a firm that he could not ordinarily afford.

Beyond the practical aspects of the project, the booklet was also my first look at the editorial form of self-promotion; that is, the piece was conceived, written, designed, and illustrated as an independent essay. It was meant to be of general

Facing page: Covers from the Herring Design Quarterly.

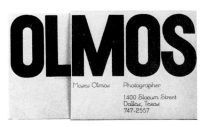
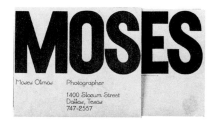

Above: The Moses Olmos business card.
Below: Hobo Signs *by Jim Jacobs.*

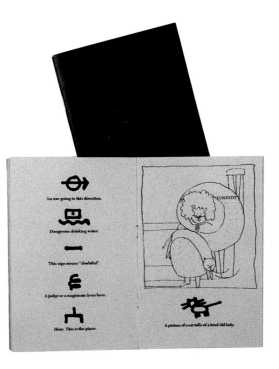

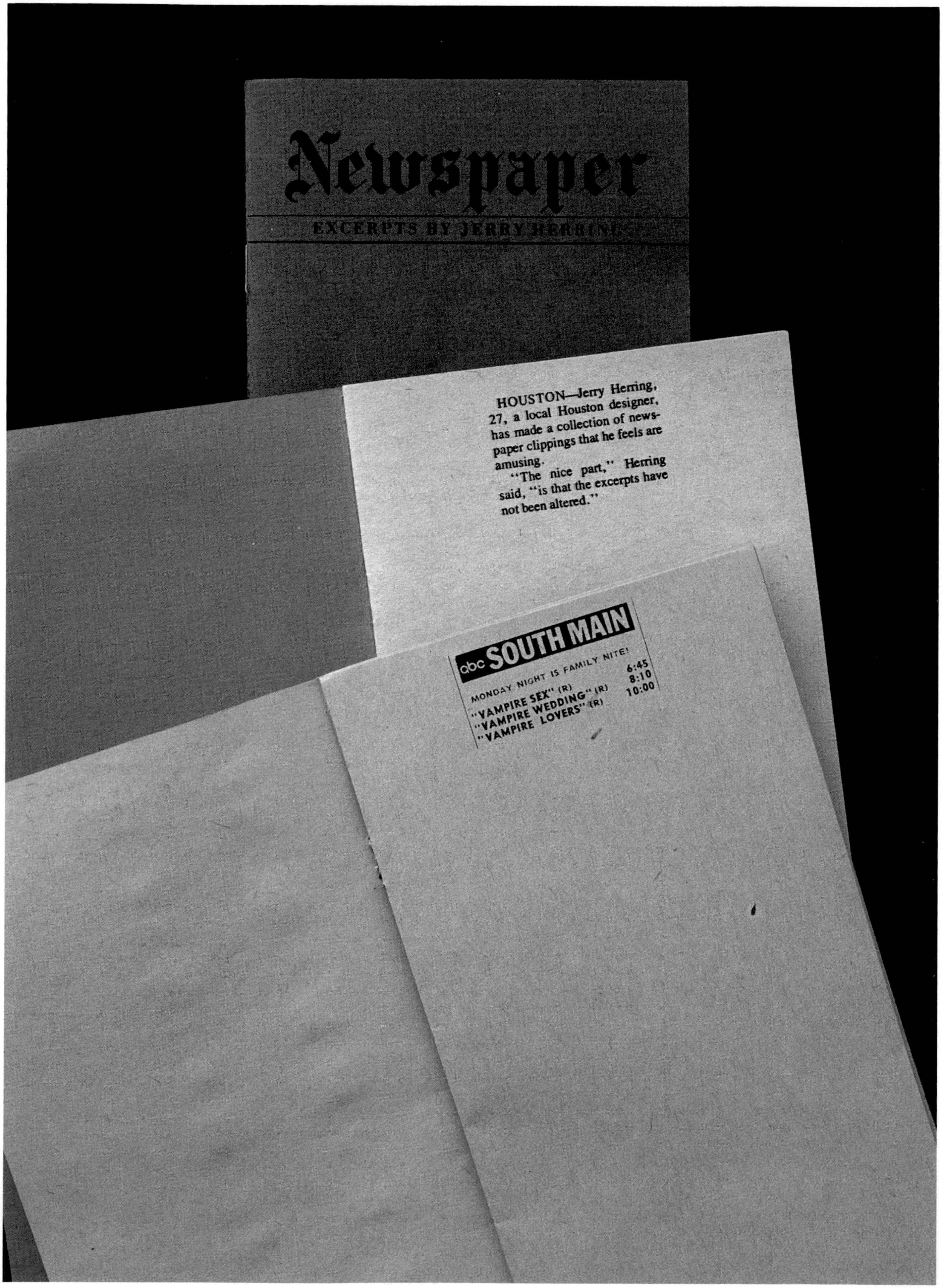

Newspaper

EXCERPTS BY JERRY HERRING

HOUSTON—Jerry Herring, 27, a local Houston designer, has made a collection of newspaper clippings that he feels are amusing.

"The nice part," Herring said, "is that the excerpts have not been altered."

abc SOUTH MAIN

MONDAY NIGHT IS FAMILY NITE!

"VAMPIRE SEX" (R)   6:45
"VAMPIRE WEDDING" (R)   8:10
"VAMPIRE LOVERS" (R)   10:00

interest and amusement to almost anyone. The booklet promoted the studio and a printer, but did not talk about them or show their work, except for the closing remarks.

I still have a copy of *Hobo Signs*, and I'm sure others do as well. What a great way to showcase your major product—creativity—by creating a work that people want to keep.

My first attempts at self-promotion were letterheads for my wife and friends. The purpose was simply to have printed items that could be entered in local art directors competitions. I was trying to express myself and at the same time seek recognition from my current employer as well as possible future employers. It was not a new tactic, by any means. Today the idea of setting up your own project and producing it is still a valid one, although today's art directors shows are nearly inundated with this type of piece. The pressure is greater than ever to create the "idea" that will make an impression.

OUT ON MY OWN

It wasn't long after I had been out on my own that I produced my first direct mail promotion. I had been collecting newspaper clippings for some time, some humorous, some just absurd. It occurred to me that the collection would make a nice little booklet along the lines of *Hobo Signs*. It would be an opportunity to send something to the art directors around town that I was trying to get in to see, and at the same time share my sense of humor with them.

Lacking any real budget for printing, I had the pages printed at a local Kwik Kopy on newsprint that I supplied. I silkscreened the covers myself before hand cutting and hand stapling the booklet together. The total cost was in the twenty-dollar range. About thirty copies were mailed out, mostly to friends and art directors I had met. (I was shy about sending the booklet to someone I had not met for fear of offending them with the humor—or lack of humor—in the piece.) After mailing the booklets, I sat back and waited for the phone to ring off the hook. It didn't.

What I found out was that a direct mail piece that does not ask for a response will not receive one. If you want people to call you, you have to ask them to.

But something else was happening here as well. When I would run into people at parties or other social occasions they would comment on the piece I sent them. They weren't dropping everything and picking up the phone to call me with work, but they were beginning to take notice. They did know that I was out there.

My second mailer was more focused. For some time I had been receiving, and saving, mail with any number of variations on my name and address. So I took the opportunity to publish the collection and make a point of what my address and phone number *actually* were. Again, no avalanche

Facing page: The cover and two spreads from the newsprint mailer, Newspaper Excerpts.

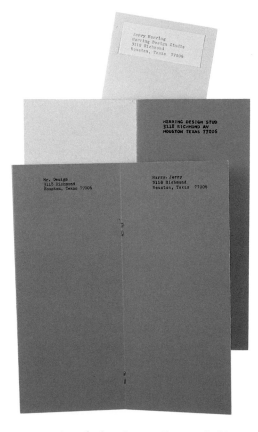

A mailer based on a collection of address labels to remind prospective clients of the studio's real address.

Stock Trade Marks

Dear corporation president, public relations director or agency art buyer: Are you in need of a dynamic new image to replace the smoking smoke stacks you or your client is now using as a trade mark? Well, I'm sure the answer to that question is YES! But you're hesitant to act because of the time, expense and uncertainty of selecting an image to represent you or your client.

That is precisely why Herring Design Studio of Houston, Texas has gone to the effort of preparing this collection of Stock Trade Marks. Long a leader in the design of trade marks and logotypes, HDS now draws on this vast experience to offer trade marks that are not only inexpensive, but can be used for almost any company.

So why not order a trade mark today? You may want to order one for yourself and all your subsidiaries.

When ordering, specify the full name of the company and whether you want the trade mark centered over the name or to the right side. All the designs are available in black, green and blue. A few are available in red. Allow 2-3 weeks for delivery.

The World Trade Mark. Very versatile, although you should have at least one out-of-state office.

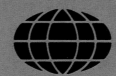

The Arrow Trade Mark. For companies on the move, on the way up or on the go. Specify if you are going straight up or to the right.

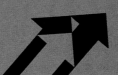

The Eagle Trade Mark. An excellent choice for patriotic firms. A big favorite among banks, for some reason. Specify brown or bald.

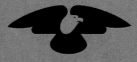

The Crest Trade Mark. Has a quiet dignity. Especially good for new restaurants in need of a long history.

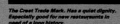

_____ *I would like to order Trade Mark number _____*
_____ *Although I certainly like what you have here, I've got a bundle to drop and would like you to custom design a trade mark for me.*
_____ *I am going to sue you because my trade mark appears on page _____*

For a booklet of original trade mark designs, please call or write:

Herring Design
3118 Richmond Avenue
Houston, Texas 77098
522-3400

of calls. But now when I would call someone, my call would actually be returned.

The third was even more direct. I had been building a growing trademark portfolio, and I thought the time was right to put together a booklet of my marks. This was my first attempt at a "portfolio" piece, and it was to be a real challenge. First, I had to come clean in the booklet that some of the marks had been designed while I was with other design firms. This is always a problem when starting out in business when the work you have to show was produced as an employee. I decided to handle this up front (see illustration). Again I used an inexpensive printer who printed flat sheets that I later cut, folded, and stitched myself. Making them by hand allowed me to add something extra. I used an imbossing die and stamped the cover with a wax seal that read "Trade Marks." To add even a little more variation, I constantly used new flysheets. The brochure was a very successful tool for me for a long time, and one that I gave out as fast as I could hand make them.

But then, paydirt! My fourth self-promotion booklet pulled the type of response that a freelancer dreams of. *Stock Trademarks* was a humorous look at trademark design and it hit a collective nerve in the advertising and design communities. Maybe it was because the parody was so close to the truth, or maybe it was because *Communication Arts* magazine ran the entire brochure in one of its issues. But whatever it was, the phone started ringing and the letters came in. Letters from Keokuck, Iowa and Prague, Czechoslovakia. Calls from across town and across the country. Some callers thought the piece wonderfully on target, others thought that it was actually a serious effort and wanted my "stock trademark" price list. It was a wonderful, funny time. And, as should have been the case, calls for my design work increased.

HERRING DESIGN QUARTERLY

Now I was hooked. It was time to get serious about maintaining an image. So in the footsteps of such firms as Pentagram and Pushpin, I dauntlessly began the *Herring Design Quarterly*.

The *Quarterly* has proved to be a good vehicle. Giving it a consistent size from the start helped to focus the series on ideas as opposed to format. Maintaining a mailing list also helped to keep the concepts for the booklets as broad as possible. And I have had to sharpen my editorial skills to make sure the subject matter, as well as the design of the booklets, is interesting.

Before I begin a *Quarterly*, I ask myself: "Will most of the people on my list appreciate what is in this booklet?" I have to remind myself that the people I want to make an impression on, my clients and prospects, are people who read, who are intuitive, and who recognize quality. They usually can't differentiate between Garamond and Helvetica,

Facing page: Spreads from the Stock Trade Marks *mailer.*

Above: The opening spread from the first portfolio mailing. The copy points out that some of the work was done while at other studios.

Below: A poster of trade marks that was mailed to advertising agencies. At the time of this mailer the bulk of the studio's work was from agencies.

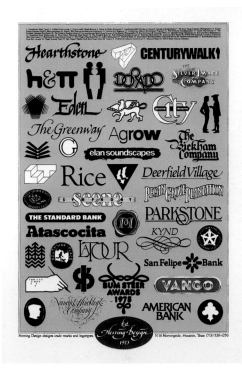

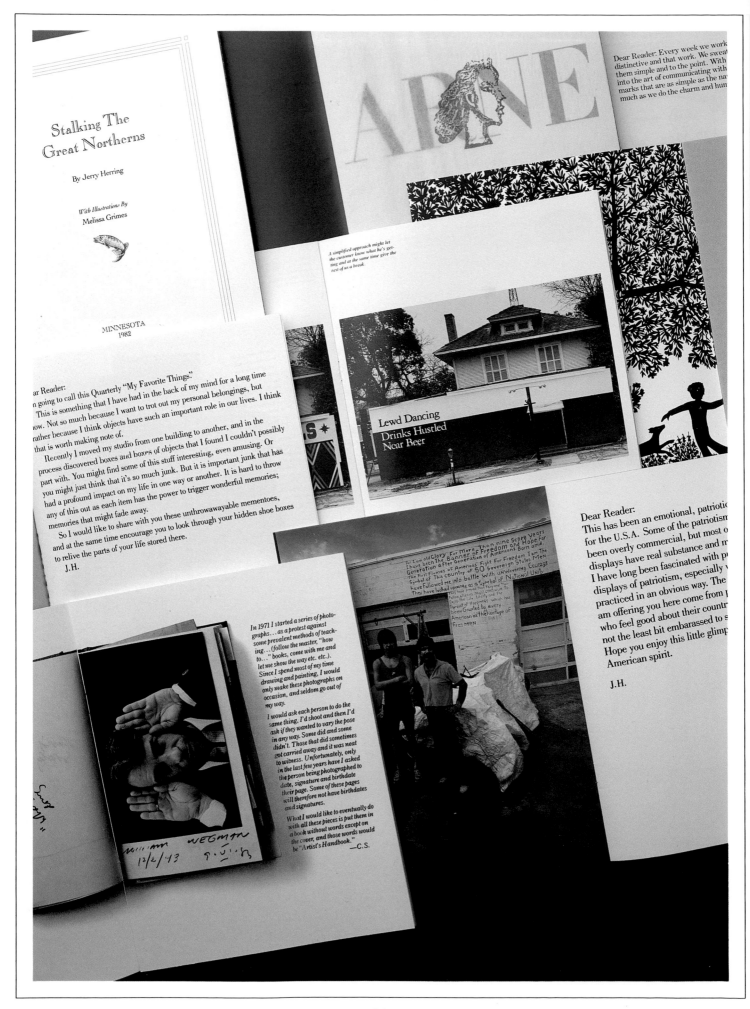

Stalking The
Great Northerns

By Jerry Herring

With Illustrations By
Melissa Grimes

MINNESOTA
1982

Dear Reader:
I'm going to call this Quarterly "My Favorite Things."
This is something that I have had in the back of my mind for a long time
now. Not so much because I want to trot out my personal belongings, but
rather because I think objects have such an important role in our lives. I think
that is worth making note of.

Recently I moved my studio from one building to another, and in the
process discovered boxes and boxes of objects that I found I couldn't possibly
part with. You might find some of this stuff interesting, even amusing. Or
you might just think that it's so much junk. But it is important junk that has
had a profound impact on my life in one way or another. It is hard to throw
any of this out as each item has the power to trigger wonderful memories;
memories that might fade away.

So I would like to share with you these unthrowawayable mementoes,
and at the same time encourage you to look through your hidden shoe boxes
to relive the parts of your life stored there.

J.H.

A simplified approach might let
the customer know what he's getting and at the same time give the
rest of us a break.

Lewd Dancing
Drinks Hustled
Near Beer

In 1971 I started a series of photographs... as a protest against
some prevalent methods of teach-
ing... (follow the master, "how
to..." books, come with me and
let me show the way etc. etc.).
Since I spend most of my time
drawing and painting, I would
only make these photographs on
occasion, and seldom go out of
my way.

I would ask each person to do the
same thing, I'd shoot and then I'd
ask if they wanted to vary the pose
in any way. Some did and some
didn't. Those that did sometimes
got carried away and it was neat
to witness. Unfortunately, only
in the last few years have I asked
the person being photographed to
date, signature and birthdate
their page. Some of these pages
will therefore not have birthdates
and signatures.

What I would like to eventually do
with all these pieces is put them in
a book without words except on
the cover, and those words would
be "Artist's Handbook."
—C.S.

Dear Reader: Every week we work
distinctive and that work. We swea
them simple and to the point. With
into the art of communicating with
marks that are as simple as the nav
much as we do the charm and hum

Dear Reader:
This has been an emotional, patrioti
for the U.S.A. Some of the patriotism
been overly commercial, but most o
displays have real substance and m
I have long been fascinated with p
displays of patriotism, especially
practiced in an obvious way. The
am offering you here come from
who feel good about their countr
not the least bit embarassed to s
Hope you enjoy this little glimp
American spirit.

J.H.

WILLIAM WEGMAN
12/2/73

but they are interested in interesting items and quickly bored by ill-conceived work.

The quarterlies that seem to elicit the most response are the ones that have some emotional content. I have received numerous letters and calls when I talk about family, such as a *Quarterly* on a fishing trip with my father and two brothers, or one in which I shared letters that I have saved over the years. Frequently, we become so involved in the business of what we do that we may forget that the people we want to work for are moved by the same feelings that move us. We have an advantage because we have the skills to communicate these feelings.

Other quarterlies that have been especially well received have been slightly humorous, such as the *Quarterly* in which I proposed design schemes for pornographic bars and theaters. This particular booklet was reprinted by the city magazine, and drew comment from the mayor.

For the booklets to be successful, they have to be treated as a regular job. I spend time conceiving, designing, and writing each piece, and I schedule time to make sure that once the project has begun, it will be finished. (It is frustrating to start a promotion piece and then let its production lapse so long that interest in the piece is lost.)

ANNUAL REVIEW

The last step, so far, on this promotional staircase was coming to terms with a continuing portfolio piece. Herring Design is now an established firm that receives regular calls for samples. This is flattering, of course, but also time-consuming and expensive. Expensive because many of the samples themselves are expensive. Many design firms have capabilities brochures, and for years I tried to come to grips with how to do one of these. The major stumbling block for me was that we were always involved with a project that I felt might be the best thing we had ever done. How could I justify producing a capabilities brochure and not include our most wonderful, most recent project? Well, I couldn't, so nothing was ever done.

Finally, while producing an annual report for a client, the idea of doing an annual report for *my* firm became a clear compromise to the problem of timeliness. At first I was reluctant, because I wasn't sure I could adequately fill an annual review. And I knew if I started an "annual" review I would have to continue it. Other firms, such as Pentagram, mailed annual reviews, but they were much larger firms. Eventually, I decided that the advantage of having a yearly document with the latest samples was worth the risk. After several issues, the idea has proved itself. My only regret is that I didn't begin producing an annual review ten years earlier. Of course, I didn't know then what I know now.

Facing page: Spreads from the Herring Design Quarterly.

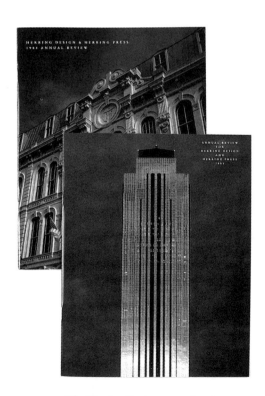

The Herring Design annual reviews recap the projects from the past year. The four-color, 36-page brochures serve as an annual mailer and as a part of new client presentations.

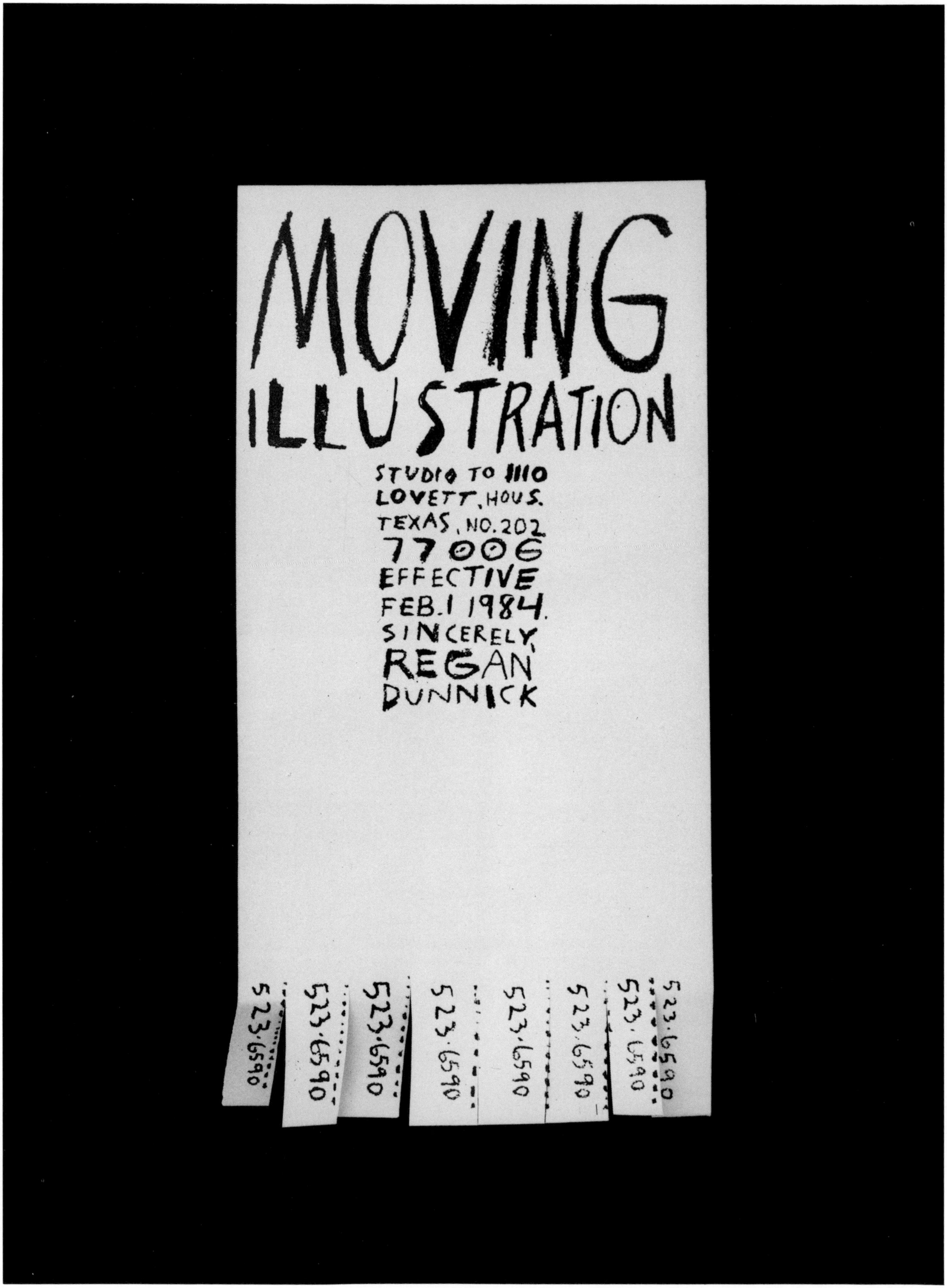
MOVING
ILLUSTRATION
STUDIO TO 1110
LOVETT, HOUS.
TEXAS, NO. 202
77006
EFFECTIVE
FEB. 1 1984.
SINCERELY,
REGAN
DUNNICK
523.6590
523.6590
523.6590
523.6590
523.6590
523.6590
523.6590
523.6590

CREATIVE PROMOTION ON A SHOESTRING

More often than not, a creative person's first self-promotion efforts will be produced on a shoestring budget. This may seem like a large problem, but in many cases it may turn out to be a real advantage. What people respond to are ideas. Good ideas.

Often with little or no budget, the idea becomes more important than the execution. Four-color printing and expensive paper stock may be replaced by one-color printing on newsprint. The idea must capture the audience's imagination. So, how can this be done?

The important thing to keep in mind is that you are promoting your own talent. So do what you do best. You can draw or take pictures or write. Fine. But what else? You need to delight or move people, or make them laugh. *You need to display the type of communication skills that you are asking them to hire you for.*

This chapter shows samples of work that have been produced on very small budgets. Illustrator Regan Dunnick corresponded with the art directors he was working for, or wished to work for, with sketches, many of which were personalized to that individual. Los Angeles designer Ken White mailed out a series of one-color postcards telling prospective clients about the work his studio was doing.

Tom Upton, a California photographer, makes postcards with photo prints and backs them with humorous copy. The effort has a double advantage. The cards are inexpensive and can be made whenever he is slow, or just when he feels the need. And the copy lets people know that he has a sense of humor. "This is basic grass roots, labor-intensive self-promotion," says Upton. "Once I have a negative I like, I print 175 to 200 postcards ($30), letterpress them with a message and a logo ($75 to $100) and label and mail them ($35). This comes to about one dollar per post card. This is less than a directory page, and I am able to let prospects see my current work soon after it happens. I am convinced that my frequent communications have a lot to do with word-of-mouth referrals."

It is not only important to get people's attention, it is also important to let them know a little bit about you. Not just about your work, about you.

Writer Jim Sanders, after nineteen years as an agency creative director, used the best—and least expensive—tool he could think of when he launched his freelance business. He wrote a letter. "It seemed sort of pointless to show all the work that I had been responsible for at the agency, and besides, I couldn't afford to anyway. I wanted people to hire me to write, so I wrote for them."

Regan Dunnick Illustration
Facing page: To announce a change of address, illustrator Regan Dunnick hand lettered a sign reminiscent of a bulletin board message, had it printed at a corner "quick printer" (in red), and sliced the paper to create the "tear-off numbers." "I spent $20 on that one," says Regan. "Well, maybe it went as high as $22. I printed about 100 copies. Some were mailed, but most were just hand delivered."
Audience: *Art directors and designers*
Description: *5″ x 8″ one-color flier*
Quantity: *100*

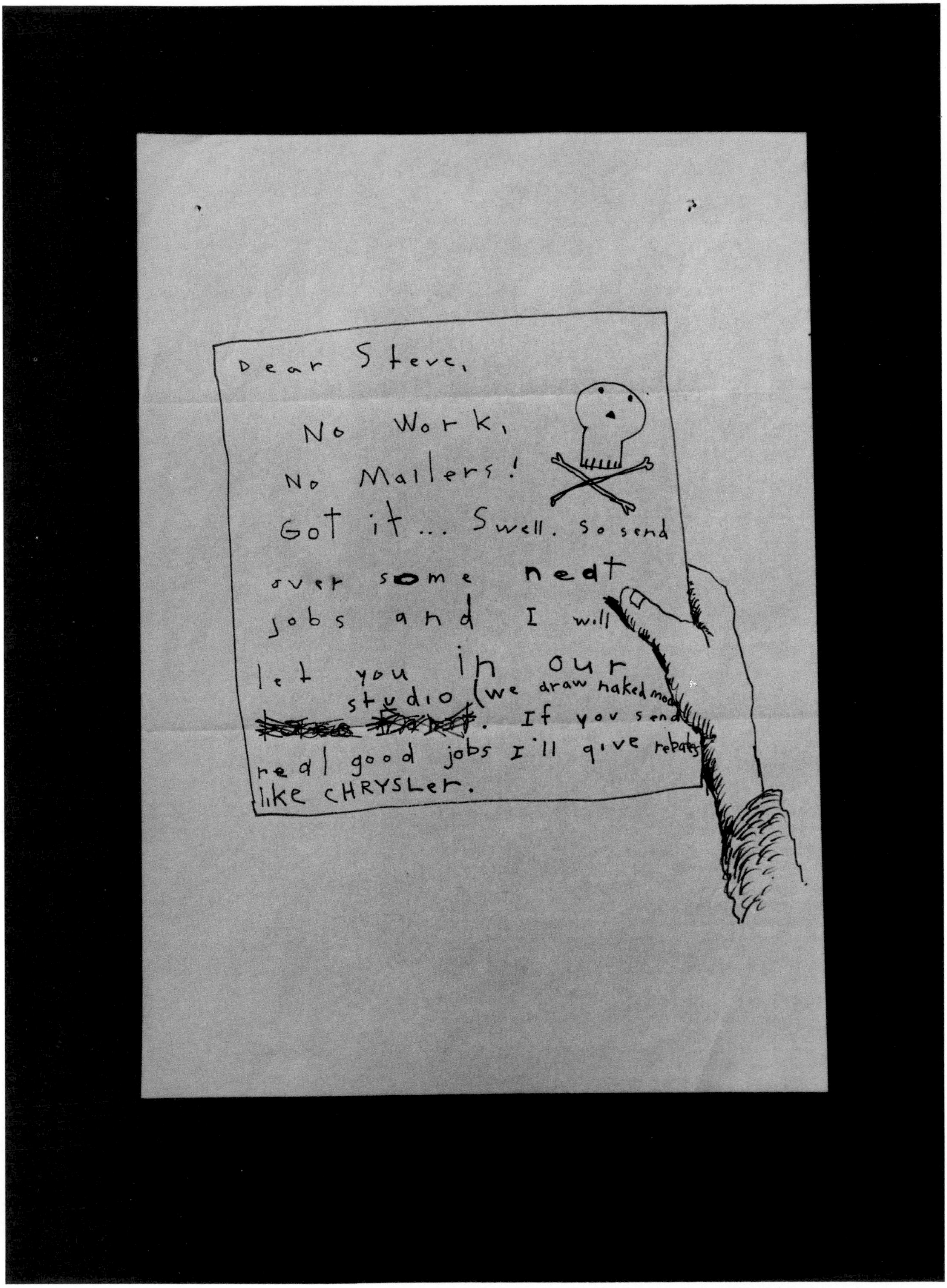
Dear Steve,
No Work,
No Mailers!
Got it... Swell. So send
over some neat
jobs and I will
let you in our
studio (we draw naked mod
. If you send
real good jobs I'll give rebates
like CHRYSLER.

Regan Dunnick Illustration

Agency art director Steve Stanley has a collection of drawings that illustrator Regan Dunnick has sent him over the years. "I would come into my office and find these," says Stanley. "They could be anything from a thank-you to a tongue-in-cheek threat to a plea for more business. They're wonderful, and the envy of other art directors who may not be on his list."

The cost of such personal self-promotion is obviously very low, while the impact on the particular client is very great.

"I couldn't afford to take the time to do these for every client," adds Regan. "Of course, some wouldn't even want me to. But I knew Steve real well, and knew that he really enjoyed the drawings. I wouldn't want to say that he 'owed me,' but I did get my share of work from him."
Audience: *Individual clients*
Description: *Custom drawings*

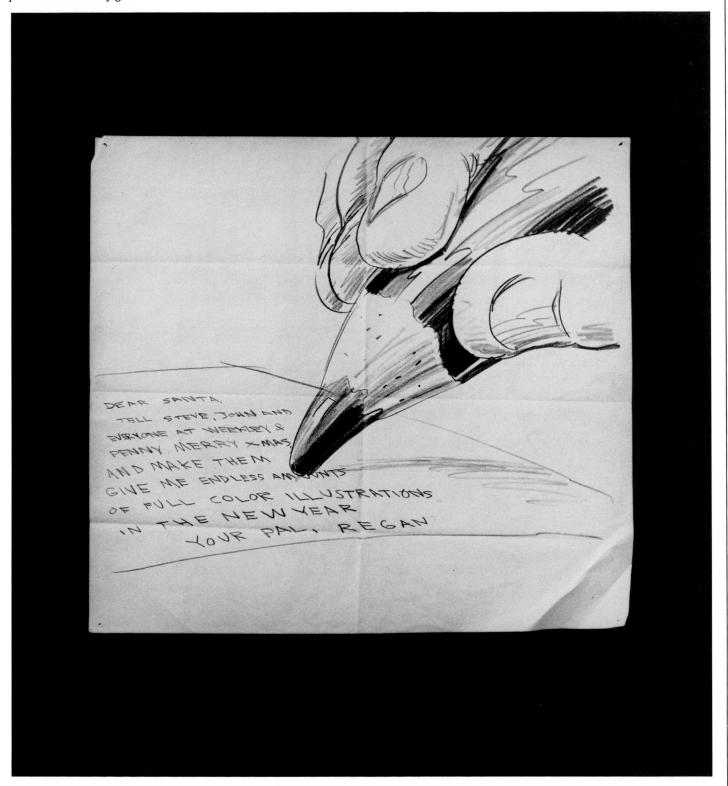

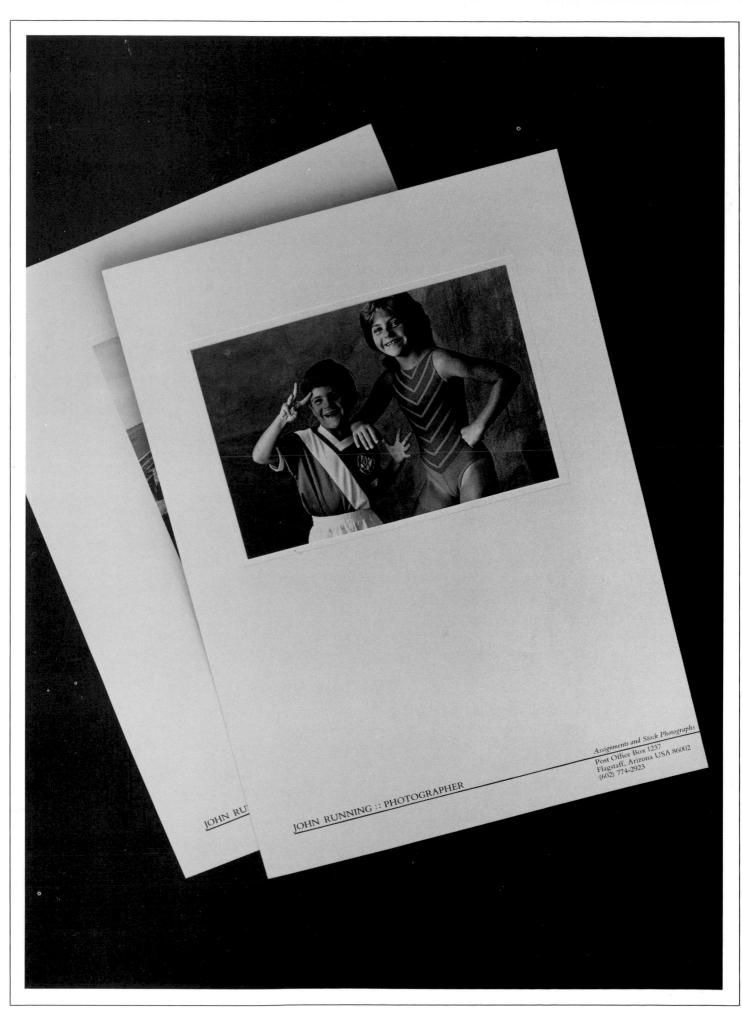

JOHN RUNNING :: PHOTOGRAPHER

Assignments and Stock Photographs
Post Office Box 1237
Flagstaff, Arizona USA 86002
(602) 774-2923

John Running, Photographer

Photographer John Running uses a preprinted card on which he adheres photo prints. The images shown here are black and white, although the format allows John to use color prints as well. A letter is included with the cards that serves as a business pitch and a caption for the photographs: "On location or in the studio, a photographer needs to be able to work anywhere and John Running works everywhere. He spent two weeks on an island in the Sea of Cortez photographing a Mexican fishing family and an hour photographing a brother and sister in his studio in Flagstaff, Arizona. Both series of photographs work."

John spends about $1.50 to $2 apiece for the mailings, including postage. "I send them out to people that I really want to work with. This seems to work better than a mass-mailing."

Audience: *Advertising and corporate*
Description: *8½" x 11" cards with mounted prints*
Quantity: *100 each mailing*

McDill

Designers John McCarthy and Michael Dillion used a postcard to announce they were relocating to a historic Milwaukee building. Other than their own talent, the young firm had few resources at the time. They took the photograph and did the illustrations themselves. "We spent about $300 for the 500 cards. Remember, this was 1981 and we were just getting started."

Audience: *Corporate*
Description: *One-color postcard*
Quantity: *500*

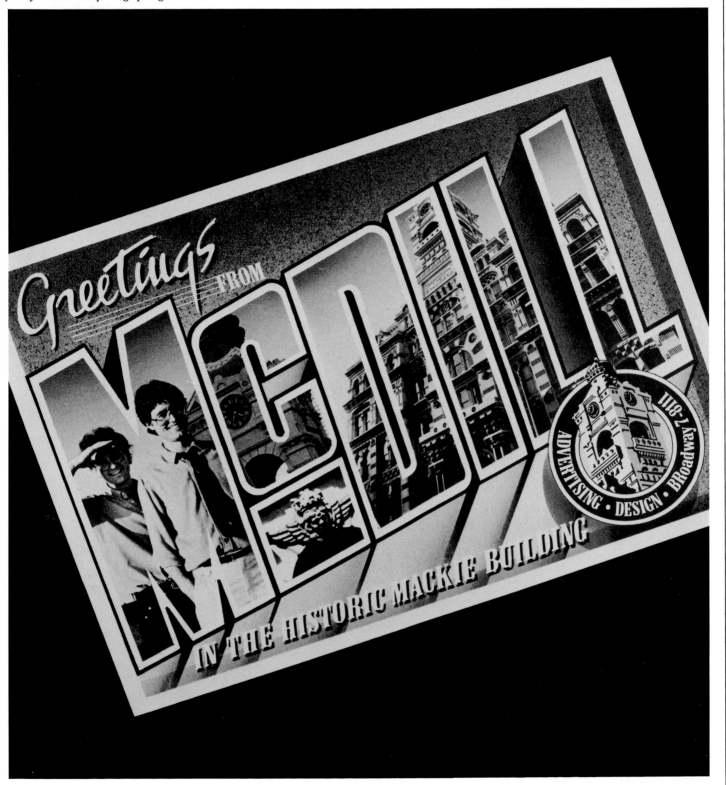

Ken White Design Office

To keep prospective clients abreast of his studio's work, Los Angeles designer Ken White sent out seven different postcards during a six-month campaign. The two-color postcards featured the line drawings of Don Weller with short, witty copy. The total budget for the project was approximately $2,100, or $300 per mailing. At first Ken sent the mailers out bulk rate, but when he discovered few people were receiving the cards, he switched to first class postage.

Audience: *Corporate and advertising*
Description: *Two color 4" x 5" postcards*
Quantity: *800 per mailing*

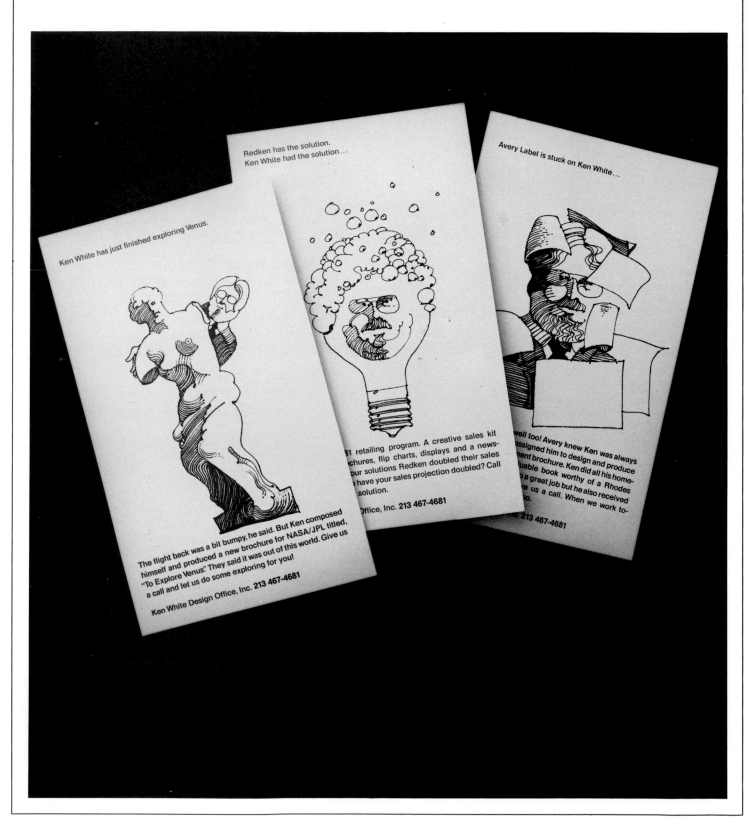

Thomas Upton Photography

Photographer Tom Upton uses handmade postcards to mail to his 175-member list. Tom selects his favorite images and makes photo prints in his lab, then has the postcard "side" letterpressed. The cards, which cost an average of $1 apiece, are mailed on a near-monthly basis.

To keep track of the people on his mailing list, Tom sends out a return card. Accompanying the reply card (right) was a postcard (shown below, upper right) with this copy:

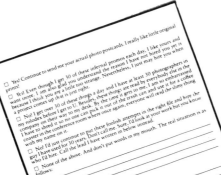

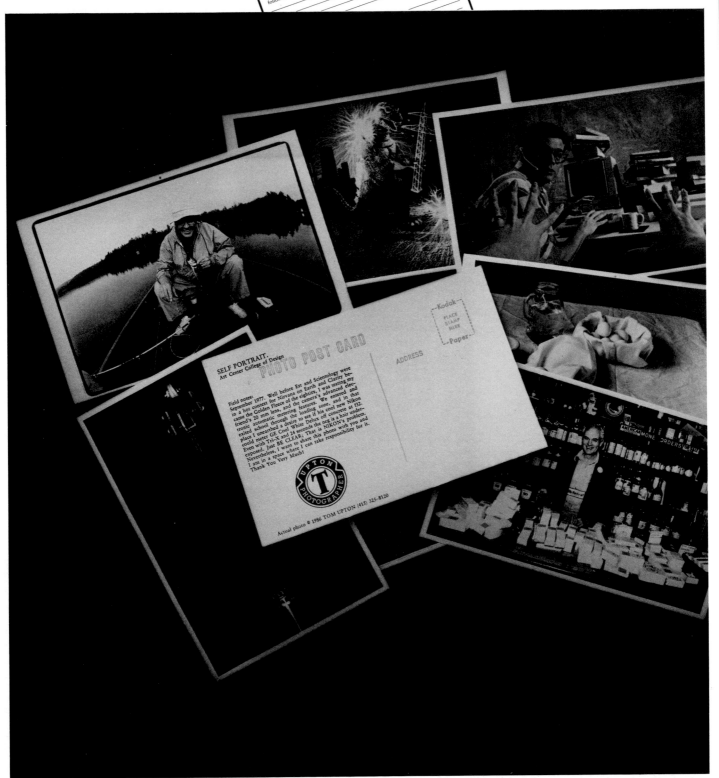

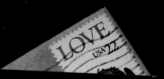

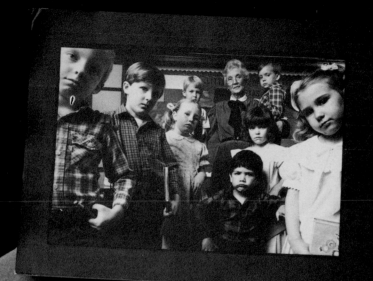

Ever felt like the New kid in town? Randy Allbritton Photography 661-1098

Randy Allbritton Photography

Photographer Randy Allbritton used handmade cards to announce his new business. "I didn't have much to spend, so I printed the photographs two up on 8" x 10" paper, mounted and trimmed them individually. I made the envelopes out of paper bags from the grocery store. For the eighty or so that I mailed out, the per-unit cost was right around $1.20. Including postage."

For Randy, the response to the mailings was immediate. "I received quite a few calls right away. I guess people responded to the feeling that the cards evoked. Everyone has been in that situation, just starting out and feeling pretty alone."

Audience: *Art directors and designers*
Description: *Handmade prints*
Quantity: *80*

Lonestar Studio

After a year and a half of being with a design firm, illustrator Larry McEntire sent out handmade fans to announce that he was reopening his illustration studio. "I printed about a hundred of the fans, had them die-cut and then glued them together myself. I got the sticks —tongue depressors—from a friend. All together they cost about $100. Another friend of mine, writer Guy Bommarito, wrote the copy."

Audience: *Art directors and designers*
Description: *8" x 5" fans*
Quantity: *100*

After a year and a half's absence, Larry McEntire and Lonestar Studio are back doing the kind of award winning illustration that's acquired them fans from coast to coast.
Call (512)476-5535 or look for the star at 2200 Rio Grande, Austin, Texas 78705.
And let them make a fan out of you.

LONESTAR IS MAKING FANS AGAIN.

Bob Scott, Illustrator

Everything you would want to know about New York illustrator Bob Scott is included in this laminated menu. The promotion piece was made just after his graduation, and included such information as projects, awards, and mechanical capabilities. "It was part of a school project at Virginia Commonwealth. I spent about $150 on the project, which was a lot of money at the time."

Audience: *Art directors and designers*
Description: *4¼" x 10½" laminated folder*
Quantity: *200*

Hungry Dog Studio

The Dog Bite, a magazine-format mailer, is photocopied, hand-colored, stapled together and mailed to a list of art directors by the illustrators Bob and Val Tillery, who make up the Hungry Dog Studio. The twelve-page mailer is designed with an editorial format, and even includes a page for a "guest artist," an illustrator who is not with the studio.

Audience: *Art directors and designers*
Description: *Stapled, photocopied, hand-colored sheets*
Quantity: *175*

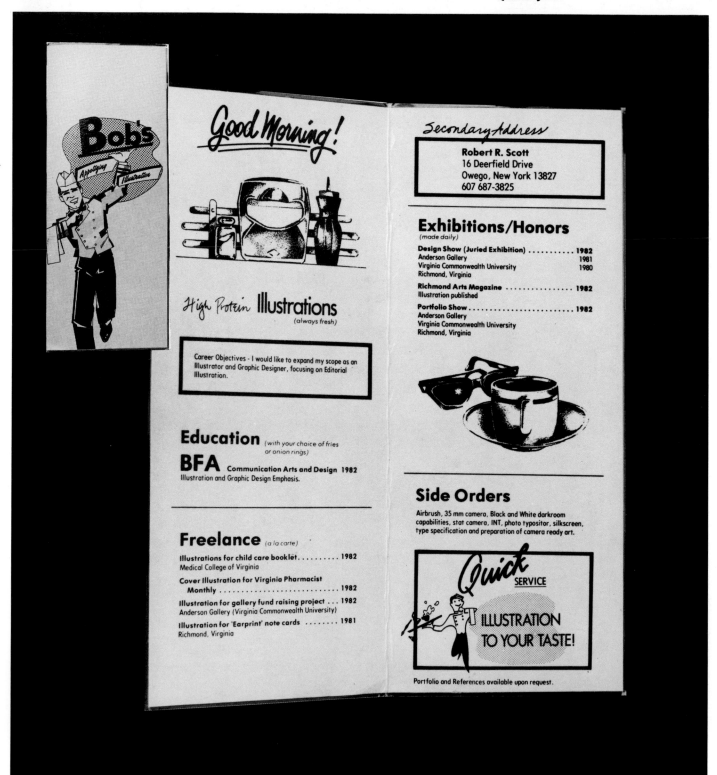

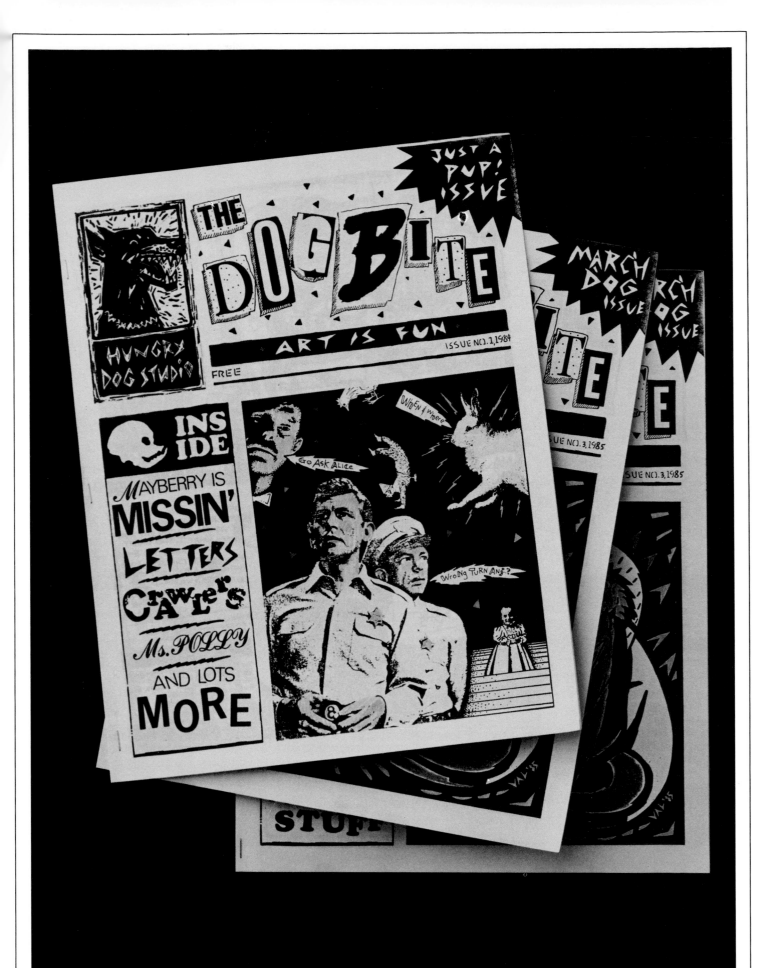

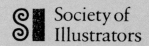

Society of Illustrators

128 East 63rd Street
New York, N.Y. 10021
212-838-2560

Regan Dunnick
3055 Walnut Bend Lane
Houston, TX 77042

November 9, 1983

Dear Mr. Dunnick,

GOLD *NOT REALLY*

On behalf of the Society of Illustrators I wish to extend congratulations
to you for winning a ~~SILVER MEDAL~~ in the INSTITUTIONAL category of the 26th
Annual National Exhibition. The award winning work is listed below.

The art director and client will be presented a SILVER MEDAL CERTIFICATE.
Awards are given only if the original art is available for hanging in the
exhibition. If you wish to purchase additional medals, please contact the
Society.

You are cordially invited to attend the Champagne Preview for the Advertising and Institutional categories on Tuesday, March 13, 1984 from 5:30 to
7:30 PM as the Society's guest. Your award will be presented to you at
that time. Kindly respond by filling and returning the enclosed form as
soon as possible.

Again, congratulations! We look forward to presenting this award to you
personally. *ALSO PLEASE BRING YOUR DOG, THANKS.*

Sincerely,

D.L. Cramer
President

I MIGHT BE IN THE NEXT WORKSHOP

1959 All Star Game / Steve Sessions / Fidelity Printing

BERNIE *BOB* *MARK* *ACE* *MY DOG* *ME*

Regan Dunnick Illustration

Illustrator Regan Dunnick photocopied a letter that he received telling him of an award in the Society of Illustrators annual exhibit, and drew over it with a colored pencil. The copies were personalized and mailed to art directors. Because the recipients knew the illustrator and his humor, this very specialized approach was effective.

Audience: *Art directors and designers*
Description: *Drawing on copy of letter*
Quantity: *10*

Jim Sanders Creative

Letters can be very effective, as well as inexpensive. The letter by writer Jim Sanders is written in a conversational tone. Although very short, Sander's letter gives a lot of insight into his experience and his writing style. Jim used a mailing service to word process the 150 personalized letters, then signed each one. To make sure that the letter didn't have the appearance of a mass-mailer, Jim licked

commemorative stamps for each envelope rather than use a postage meter.
Audience: *Advertising and corporate*
Description: *Letter*
Quantity: *150*

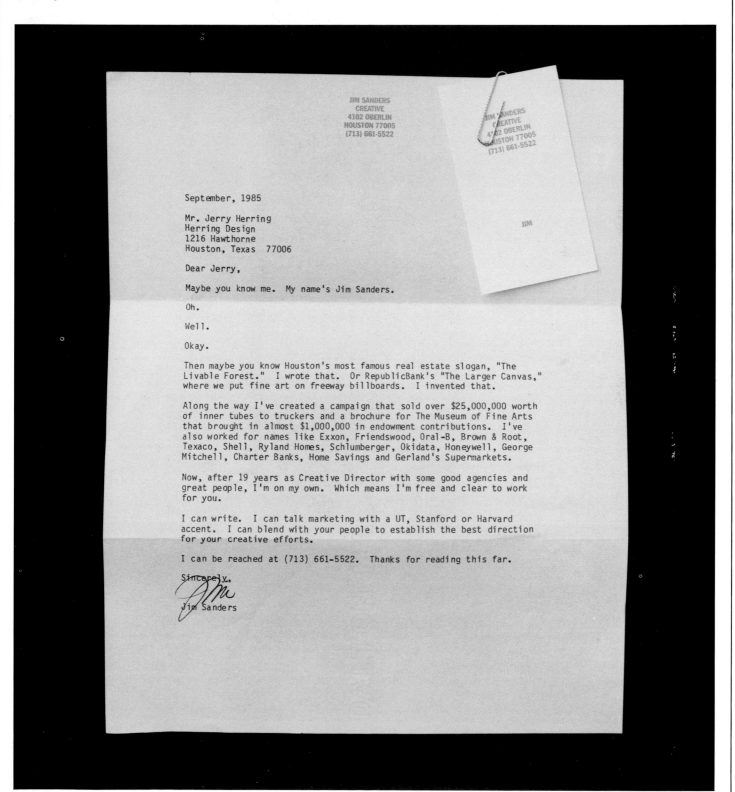

September, 1985

Mr. Jerry Herring
Herring Design
1216 Hawthorne
Houston, Texas 77006

Dear Jerry,

Maybe you know me. My name's Jim Sanders.

Oh.

Well.

Okay.

Then maybe you know Houston's most famous real estate slogan, "The Livable Forest." I wrote that. Or RepublicBank's "The Larger Canvas," where we put fine art on freeway billboards. I invented that.

Along the way I've created a campaign that sold over $25,000,000 worth of inner tubes to truckers and a brochure for The Museum of Fine Arts that brought in almost $1,000,000 in endowment contributions. I've also worked for names like Exxon, Friendswood, Oral-B, Brown & Root, Texaco, Shell, Ryland Homes, Schlumberger, Okidata, Honeywell, George Mitchell, Charter Banks, Home Savings and Gerland's Supermarkets.

Now, after 19 years as Creative Director with some good agencies and great people, I'm on my own. Which means I'm free and clear to work for you.

I can write. I can talk marketing with a UT, Stanford or Harvard accent. I can blend with your people to establish the best direction for your creative efforts.

I can be reached at (713) 661-5522. Thanks for reading this far.

Sincerely,

Jim Sanders

JIM SANDERS
CREATIVE
4102 OBERLIN
HOUSTON 77005
(713) 661-5522

Bruce, Henry & Davis

Writer Bruce Henry Davis has been staging going out of business parties for over ten years. "Well, it started as a real going out of business party, but when I didn't go out of business, I kept right on having the parties. They are something of an institution now, and besides, I like writing the invitations."

Audience: *Local advertising community*
Description: *Invitation*
Quantity: *900*

And, now, another chapter in the continuing saga of Bruce Henry Davis Advertising.

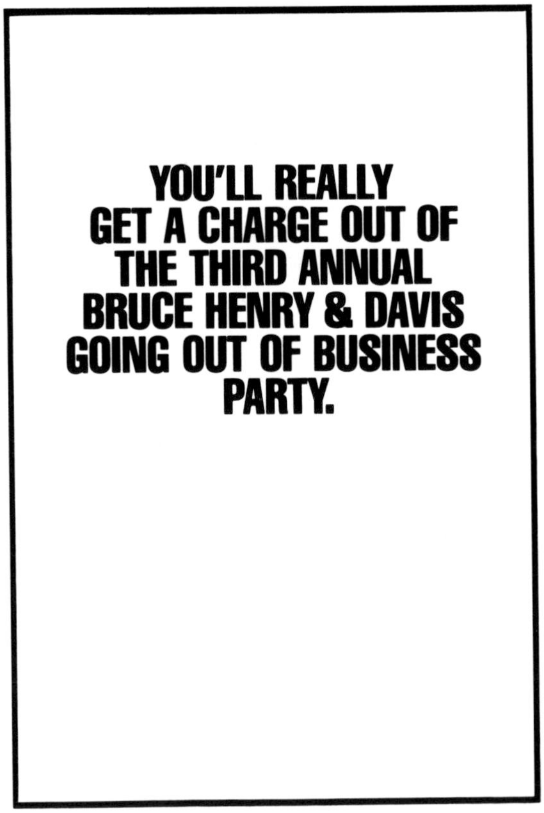

YOU'LL REALLY
GET A CHARGE OUT OF
THE THIRD ANNUAL
BRUCE HENRY & DAVIS
GOING OUT OF BUSINESS
PARTY.

1745 **LEGAL NOTICES**

BRUCE HENRY DAVIS ADVERTISING CONSULTANT HEREBY GIVES NOTICE TO CREDITORS, CUSTOMERS AND ACQUAINTANCES OF HIS LAWFUL INTENT TO DECLARE CHAPTER 11 PURSUANT TO THE CONTINUANCE OF HIS ANNUAL GOING-OUT-OF-BUSINESS PARTY, ON THURSDAY OCTOBER 4, 1984, 8 PM-2 AM, AT FITZGERALD'S, 2706 WHITE OAK AT STUDEWOOD IN THE HEIGHTS. This notice constitutes a summons to parties seeking action that they appear before the bar at said premises and move that the party of the first part be held liable for gratis draft beer, and that he present, on demand, musical exhibit A, Dr. Rockit & The Sisters of Mercy; exhibit B, Ezra Charles; and exhibit C, The Shuffle Brothers. Furthermore, it is hereby affirmed that admittance to these proceedings is decreed to be at no expense to the bearer upon presentation of this printed notice or reasonable facsimile thereof. Without the aforesaid document in hand, the constabulary of Fitzgerald's may adjudicate a $5 admission surcharge. Know all ye by this affidavit that your attendance is summoned ipso facto.

FOR LAYMAN'S TRANSLATION, PLEASE LIFT LEGAL NOTICE.

YOUR CHARGE:

Thank You!

DATE	WAITER NO.	AMOUNT	GUEST CHECK NO.
8/20/76	BRAD	1.00	38233

CUSTOMER'S RECEIPT — Keep above record for income tax or expense account, if needed + detach below this line.

TABLE NO.	WAITER NO.	PERSONS	GUEST CHECK NO.
3	BRAD	1	38233

1 Going out of
business party
donation   1.00

Gratuity not included

TAX

STYLE
58CB   PLEASE PAY CASHIER

For the third year in a row, advertising's funkiest affair and most questionable tax deduction promises to be bigger than ever.

So big, in fact, that this could well be the going out of business party that actually puts Bruce Henry & Davis Advertising out of business.

So, when we ask you to this year's party, that's not all we're asking.

As you walk in the door at Liberty Hall on August 20, there will be a small, unobtrusive bucket in which you may drop a dollar or any other donation you care to make.

(Should you have difficulty locating the bucket, simply ask the large, tattooed gentleman who will also be positioned just inside the door.)

You couldn't contribute to a worthier cause.

You'll be kindly rewarded with all the beer and set-ups you can drink.

You'll hear the romp-stomping music of the Hemmer Ridge Mountain Boys, who've just signed a contract with Capitol Records (for five free records and one record a month at $9.99).

And you can count on additional, out of the ordinary amusement to make this a night you won't forget, even if you do have trouble remembering it the next morning.

To keep out gate-crashing groupies, please bring this invitation with you for admission. Otherwise, Bruce will have to come to the door and identify you, and then who'll run the projector?

Please come in a charitable spirit to the third annual Bruce Henry & Davis going out of business party at Liberty Hall, Friday, August 20, 7:30 PM-1:00 AM.

This year we're going for broke.

Special thanks to Words & Things and Oak Creek Press for donating their typography and printing services, although we'd have preferred cash.

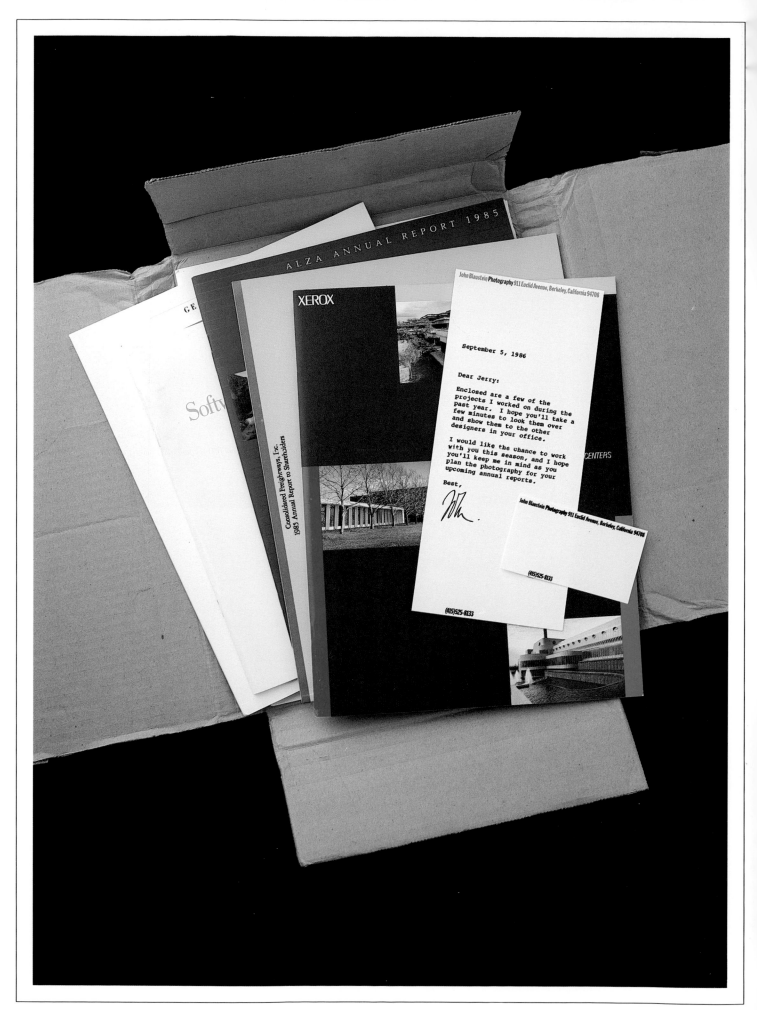

ASKING FOR THE BUSINESS

Many self-promotion efforts eventually find themselves in the pages of advertising, design, or photography annuals. Sometimes these pieces are honored because they are good communication tools. Other times they are in these annuals only because they "look good." When designing self-promotion programs, we often lose sight of the ultimate goal, which is to get work. At some point in the process of promoting, you must *ask* for the business.

Asking for the business can be an element in many different forms. It can be part of an expensive promotion, or it can be a simple statement in a letter. The important point here is that somewhere, somehow, you need to come right out and say:

"I would appreciate the opportunity to bid on your future projects…"

"Please keep me in mind when planning your next annual report…"

"I feel that we could contribute to your overall image and would appreciate the opportunity to demonstrate our capabilities to you…"

"We would like to show you how effective this firm can be…"

"Please look over the work we have done. I would appreciate five minutes of your time to explain how we could work together…"

"If you like what you see here, give me a call…"

Usually the best time to directly ask for the business is the first time that you correspond with a potential client. You may be showing them some of your work, or telling them something about your capabilities. The potential client forms an opinion of your work at that time. "I like to ask for the work right up front," says a New York copywriter. "If they don't like what I sent the first time, they sure aren't going to take the time to read what I send out later. Most agencies I write to have plenty of ongoing work. I want them to make a snap decision and call me right then."

Keep in mind that when you ask for business, you must present a reason why the potential client should be interested in your services. If you are showing work, the visual presentation may not be compelling enough. What else do you have to offer? What is your experience, your background? Who have you worked for? What do you have to offer that is unique, or better? Have you won awards that may be impressive to your potential audience?

When marketing yourself, make a list of your best selling points, make sure the potential client is made aware of these strengths, and then ask for the business.

Brenda Walton Calligraphy and Illustration

Illustrator Brenda Walton sends out a compelling portfolio of her watercolor botanical drawings. The drawings are reproduced on soft text paper that enhance the drawing style.

The total image is very delicate, but the letter that accompanies the package is all business. "If I may answer any questions about my work, fees, or turnaround time, please give me a call."

Audience: *Art directors and designers*
Description: *6¼" x 4¼" cards with letter*
Quantity: *500*

Gary Goodwin Photography

Dallas Photographer Gary Goodwin sends out an intriguing six-panel brochure in which he begins by asking what a client wants in a photographer, follows by stating his own work ethic, and ends with an offer to wash the car of any potential clients.

Gary explains his strategy: "The brochure went out first, two weeks later a postcard sample of my work went out with a humorous note referring to the 'car wash brochure.' Two weeks later another card sample was sent. Finally, along with the last card, an index card

was sent. Every two weeks for a period of a month and a half, every art director and designer in the Dallas area heard from me."

Audience: *Art directors and designers*
Description: *Six-panel brochure, postcard and index card campaign*
Quantity: *1,000*

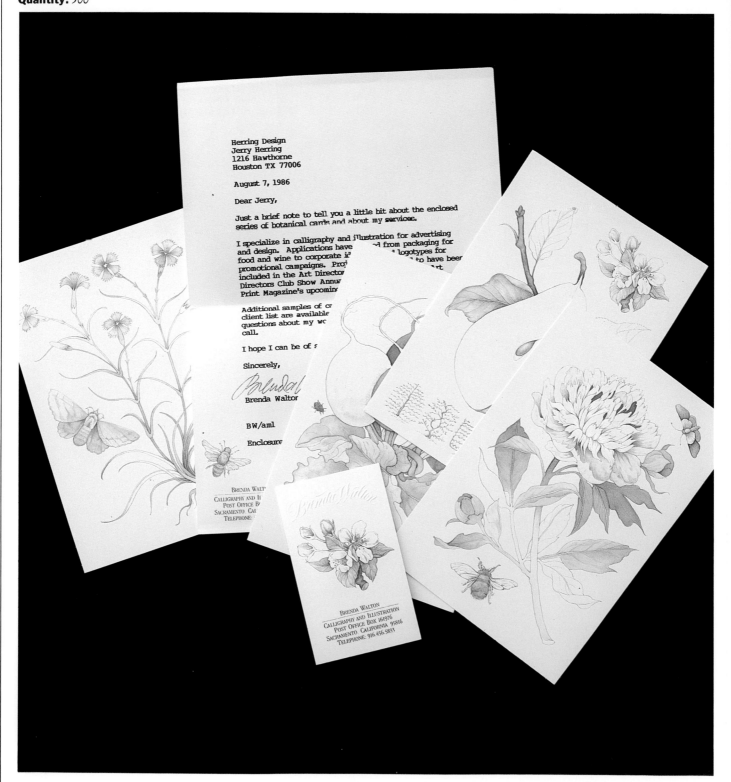

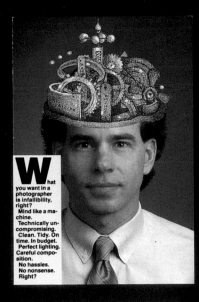

What you want in a photographer is infallibility, right?

Mind like a machine. Technically uncompromising. Clean. Tidy. On time. In budget. Perfect lighting. Careful composition.

No hassles. No nonsense. Right?

But you probably want a photographer with a sense of mischief as well — someone just a little irreverent who can put some life into what might have been just the same old images.

You don't want well-behaved docile little shots, do you?

You want pictures that bite back, right?

What you need then is a photographer who's not completely well-behaved himself.

The trouble is — as you know — that one seldom comes across both photographers in the same person at the same time.

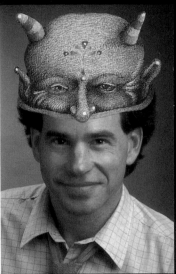

But you probably want a photographer with a sense of mischief as well — someone just a little irreverent who can put some life into what might have been just the same old images.

You don't want well-behaved docile little shots, do you?

You want pictures that bite back, right?

What you need then is a photographer who's not completely well-behaved himself.

The trouble is — as you know — that one seldom comes across both photographers in the same person at the same time.

I'm Gary Goodwin. I'm both.

A self promotion piece is no place for modesty.

I'm both.

Precise but daring. Dependable but inventive.

Naughty but nice — more or less — enough of both, at least, to wake-up your studio shots without giving you any reason to lose any sleep.

Here's how I work:

No Whining.

I'm willing to go to a lot of trouble to make your job right — after all, it's my job too — but I won't make you listen to me talk about it.

Good shots are easy for me.

And when they're not, you'll never know.

No Hassles

You have a lot of things to think about. I want your photo sessions to be smooth as glass.

If I do my job right, your biggest problem will be picking from more good shots than you have room for.

Secret Nit-Picking

By the time you get to the set, most of your job's nits will have been pre-picked.

We do the boring parts of photography in private because you should never have to stand around and watch someone tend to details that could have been taken care of an hour before you showed up.

No Surprises

That means on time and in budget with no extra charges you didn't plan on at the end of the job.

It means you get what we agreed on.

It doesn't mean you won't get an image now and then that will knock your socks off.

We believe in maximum smoothness and minimum discomfort.

And we believe in the spark.

To see the spark, you'll have to see the work.

We'll call for an appointment in the next few days.

I've been working in New York City the last few years. That makes me a semi-newcomer to Dallas. There aren't that many people you can ask about me.

I can tell you I'm a good photographer all day long, but you won't know it's so until I do that first job for you.

What's my plan to get you to give me that job?

I'll wash your car.

Really.

Call me at 631-7019 or call my rep, Molly Webb at 824-1179 and I'll come by your office and wash your car and sweep it out and check your tires and battery.

No obligation.

I promise.

My pleasure.

However.

If it turns out that you do feel a little obligated — and I suppose that's possible — well I can't stop you.

And if you give me a job because of it, you'll be glad you did anyway and you'll thank me in the long run.

So give me a call.

The very least you'll get out of it is a free car wash.

I won't be doing this for very long you know.

So call me today.

This is a limited offer.

Gary Goodwin.

Jim Jacobs' Studio

Dallas Designer Jim Jacobs realizes that most corporate clients are more verbal than visual. He produced a mailer that not only asks for work, he explains the design business, talks about the Dallas market, explains what his design firm can do for the client and how they will work together. The folder, designed as a cold-call mailer to potential corporate clients, begins by acknowledging that not every client is the same. The piece ends with a group photo (not shown).

Audience: *Corporate*
Description: *8½″ x 11″ folder*
Quantity: *1,000*

Rich Nickel Design

Rich Nickel Design, a Chicago-area design firm, has a systemized strategy for new business.

The initial mailing is a piece that asks "But does it sell?" The card is accompanied by a cover letter and a reply card to set up a meeting.

After the potential client responds and a meeting is set up, a descriptive, copy-only brochure with the cover line "If you buy our company, we'll sell yours" is sent by overnight express before the meeting takes place.

After the presentation, a sheet is left behind that states the design firm's beliefs. The total package, states Dale Janzen, results in "people who think we are crazy, or the start of a new relationship."

Audience: *Corporate*
Description: *8¾″ x 12″ card with laminated business card. 6½″ x 9″ return card. 9½″ x 12½″ twelve-page brochure. 8¾″ x 12″ follow-up card.*
Quantity: *1,000*

Read this part if you're not sure
what a design studio does
or why you got a brochure from one.

Read this part if your business is
a heck of a lot more impressive than
anyone would know by looking
and it's high time you found a good designer
but you haven't for some reason or another.

Read this part if you've been buying
design for years, you're working with someone
you're satisfied with, and it would take a lot
to get you to look at one more portfolio.

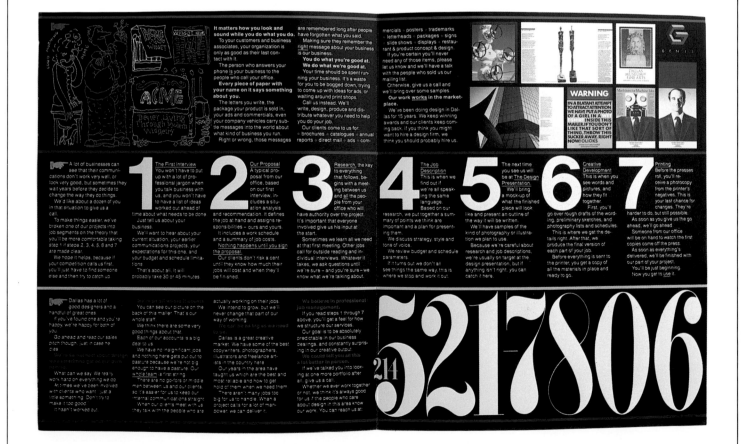

But does it sell?

You have an ad campaign. Those Other Guys put one together for you. Looks alright. Got a nice rhythm to it. Not bad. Not bad.

Now ask yourself *the* question.
(See headline.)

Well? As much as your campaign should sell? How about your corporate image or product positioning? Did they survive the budget battle? Perhaps, just perhaps, there are a few gaps.

We'd like to talk to you about your company, your goals, your needs. And some profitable solutions. Fill out the enclosed reply card. The first thing we'll bring is donuts. Then we'll begin to fill in the holes.

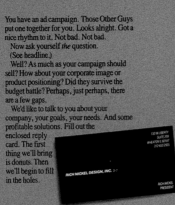

130 W LIBERTY
SUITE 209
WHEATON IL 60187
312.653.2925

RICH NICKEL DESIGN, INC.

RICH NICKEL
PRESIDENT

Before we go much further, you should know these things about us.

1. We believe that printed materials are meant to be read. We're going to do everything we can to grab attention, keep it and get results.

2. We believe that any time a company puts itself in print it must be done right, or it's wrong. A simple mailing label deserves (and will get) the same attention to detail as a major campaign.

3. We believe good work speaks louder and longer than a cheap price. Your prospect has no idea how much money or how much time it took to create a piece. They only know whether it moved them or not.

4. We believe details make or break a project. That's why we must control every aspect of the project: design, copy, art, photography and printing.

5. We believe that great work happens only with great clients. Great clients are companies that have a vision, and that have people in them who dare to do what it takes to pursue that vision. Great work is simply a great company on paper.

Rich Nickel Design, Inc.
130 W. Liberty
Suite 209
Wheaton, IL 60187
312.653.2925

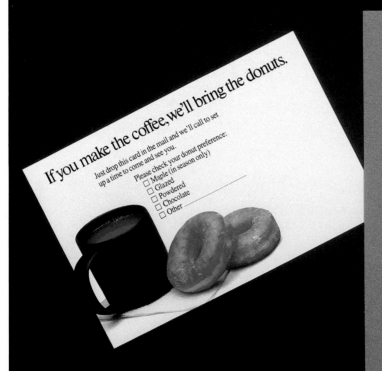

If you make the coffee, we'll bring the donuts.

Just drop this card in the mail and we'll call to set up a time to come and see you.
Please check your donut preference:
☐ Maple (in season only)
☐ Glazed
☐ Powdered
☐ Chocolate
☐ Other _____

If you buy our company, we'll sell yours.

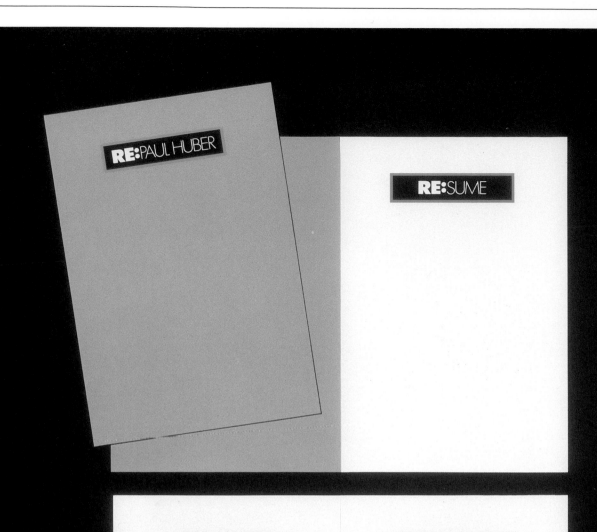

RE:PAUL HUBER

RE:SUME

RE:FERENCES

Kiku Obata and Kerry Kuehner
Creative Directors
Obata-Kuehner, Inc.
5585 Pershing Avenue
Suite 240
St. Louis, Missouri 63112
314/361-3110

Richard Deardorff
Senior Design Director
Overlock Howe Consulting Group
4484 West Pine
St. Louis, Missouri 63108
314/533-4484

Jay Loucks
Creative Director
Loucks Atelier, Inc.
2900 Weslayan
Suite 530
Houston, Texas 77027
713/877-8551

RE:VIEW

Overlock Howe & Company
St. Louis, Missouri
Graphic Designer
August 1976–November 1978

Obata-Kuehner, Inc.
St. Louis, Missouri
Art Director/Designer
November 1978–November 1980

PA & Company
Houston, Texas
Art Director/Designer
November 1980–July 1981

Loucks Atelier, Inc.
Houston, Texas
Art Director/Designer
July 1981–June 1985

Paul Huber

Designer Paul Huber took the resume to a new level with his eight-page brochure/resume. Included with the brochure was a return card.
Audience: *Design firms*
Description: *8-page brochure with reply card*
Quantity: *250*

Jo Ann Stone

Writer Jo Ann Stone has a business card that is about as direct as you can get. For people who use business cards a lot, the information the card contains can be very important. Jo Ann's not only tells what she does, but how she does it. Her letterheads have the same style, with a long copy block running down the side of the page.
Audience: *Corporate and design firms*
Description: *One-color stationery*

My name is Jo Ann Stone. I'm a writer. In fact, I write all the time.

When I'm not rewriting my business card in pursuit of new awards, I write for architects, engineers, developers, bankers, contractors, designers, and others pursuing new horizons and incomes.

If I didn't write for them, I'd probably write on walls and sidewalks — anything that let me pin thoughts down long enough to get others interested in them.

In a way, writing for a living keeps me out of trouble. My passion is to write well — not cleverly, but clearly and perceptively. It's a passion I practice.

My office address is 2472 Bolsover, Suite 365, Houston, TX 77005. The phone is 713/528-3378.

Jo Ann Stone, the writer. Oh, how Mama smiles at that.

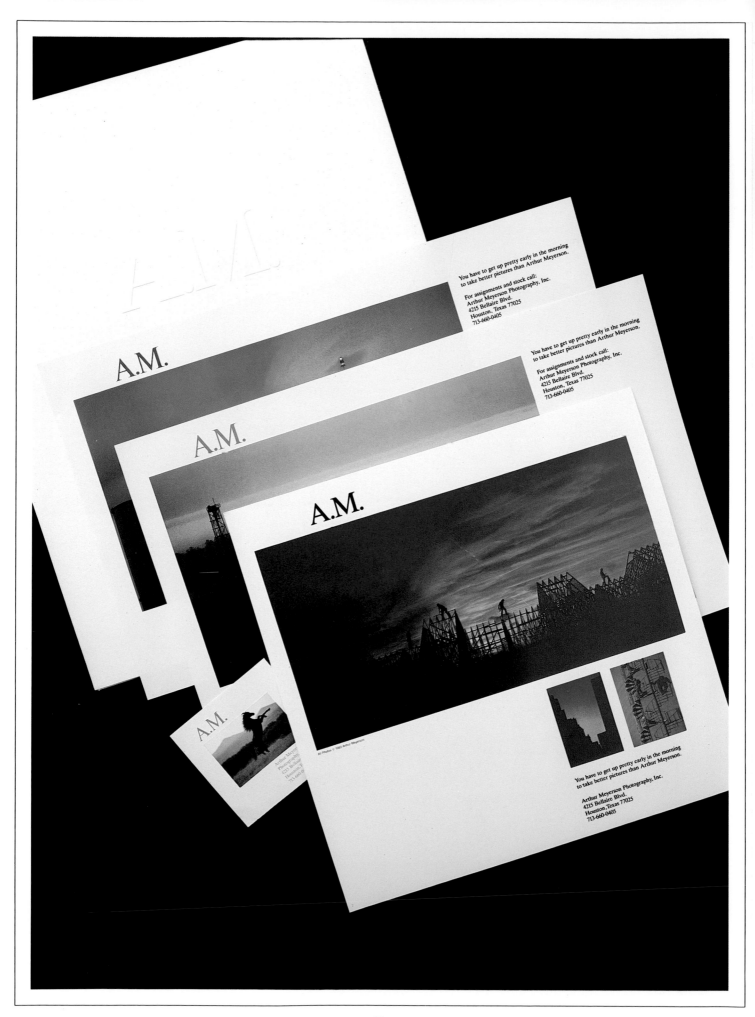

PROMOTING A TOTAL LOOK

Developing a total image for your business takes effort and determination, and a commitment of time and money. In short, what you expect from your clients.

In this chapter we look at the "coordinated campaigns" of two photographers, a writer, and a designer. The obvious success of each of these efforts is that they have been able to develop a "look."

For photographer Arthur Meyerson, the look was developed around a "concept." Working with designer Woody Pirtle, the decision was made to create an image using Arthur's initials–A.M.–because of the secondary meaning of "early morning." Arthur's marketing materials display photographs taken in early morning light and are supported by the theme line, "You have to get up pretty early in the morning to take better pictures than Arthur Meyerson."

"At first I was very reluctant to go along with Woody on using the line," admits Meyerson. "It just seemed, at the time, to be a little too promotional. But I think that it has worked very well."

Now, all of Arthur's marketing materials are coordinated with the theme line and early morning photos, including stationery and directory ads. What Arthur gives up in flexibility, he more than makes up for in memorability.

For photographer Rick Rusing, the problem of developing an image was more an answer to a portfolio problem than an advertising problem. For several years Rick and his wife/partner Terry researched ways to present their studio to prospective clients. They read, attended seminars and interviewed people for advice. Armed with a great deal of research, they hired the design firm Parker Johnson Lofgreen to design a package for them. What followed was a coordinated approach to portfolio presentations, marketing mailers and stationery (pages 52-53). For the Rusings, the look is held together with a distinctive logo and color scheme.

For writer Sam A. Angeloff and designer Craig Frazier, the look came out of a simple need. In Sam's case, stationery. In Craig's case, a direct mail piece. For these small companies, like any small company, the value of their identity will grow with each use.

Arthur Meyerson Photography
The central piece in Arthur's campaign is an award-winning poster designed for him by Woody Pirtle (below). The theme is continued with his major direct mail piece, a folder with "A.M." embossed on the cover and various four-color inserts. The look is continued with his stationery and business cards, and he follows the format with his various directory ads.
Audience: *Corporate, advertising agencies, and design firms*
Description: *Coordinated campaign: folder, inserts, stationery, director ads, and poster*
Quantity: *1,500*

Rusing Photography

Since most art directors would ask photographer Rick Rusing to "Send me your book," he produced a portfolio that was in the shape of a book (top). Inside was an introduction and duplicate portfolio transparencies. Rick developed individual portfolios in five categories: automotive, life style, travel/resort, corporate/high tech, and general.

To support the portfolio, a series of five mailers (bottom) was produced that played off the book theme. Each mailer carried a "chapter" that loosely related to a portfolio photograph. The text ended in midsentence, with the copy line on the back of the folder stating, "For the rest of the story, get the rest of the book. Call for Rick's Portfolio."

Each piece, including a Black Book© ad, carried the same graphic theme: a yellow trademark with a black background.

Audience: Art directors and designers

Description: Five 5" x 7" four-color folders

Quantity: 3,000

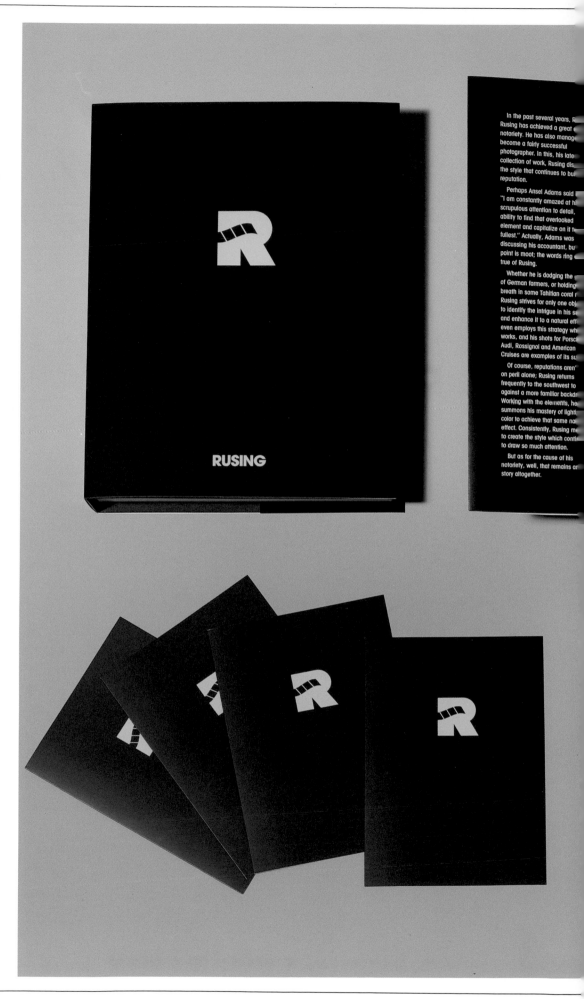

In the past several years, R Rusing has achieved a great notoriety. He has also manage become a fairly successful photographer. In this, his late collection of work, Rusing dis the style that continues to bu reputation.

Perhaps Ansel Adams said "I am constantly amazed at hi scrupulous attention to detail, ability to find that overlooked element and capitalize on it t fullest." Actually, Adams was discussing his accountant, bu point is moot; the words ring true of Rusing.

Whether he is dodging the of German farmers, or holding breath in some Tahitian coral r Rusing strives for only one obj to identify the intrigue in his s and enhance it to a natural eff even employs this strategy wh works, and his shots for Porsc Audi, Rossignol and American Cruises are examples of its su

Of course, reputations aren' on peril alone; Rusing returns frequently to the southwest to against a more familiar backdr Working with the elements, he summons his mastery of lighti color to achieve that same na effect. Consistently, Rusing m to create the style which conti to draw so much attention.

But as for the cause of his notoriety, well, that remains ar story altogether.

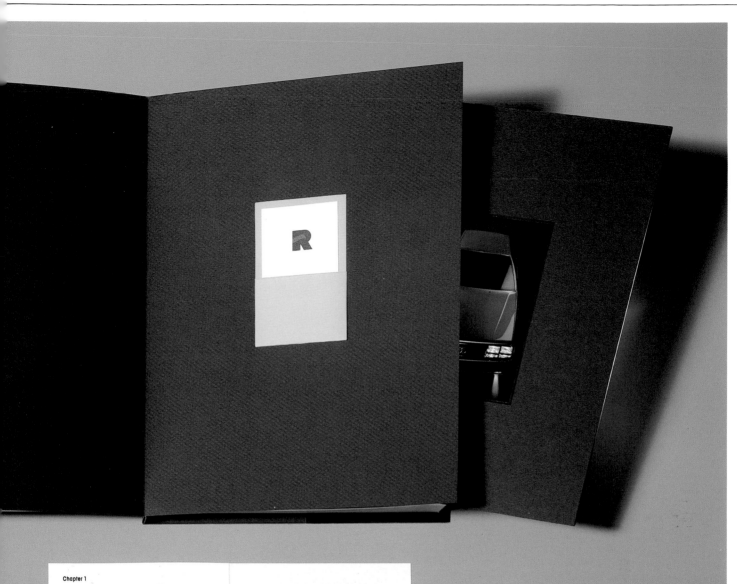

Chapter 1

Green was never my favorite color. Of course, he wasn't my favorite religion either, but that's beside the point.

It all started that summer Green and I went to Madagascar to shoot the sacred birth ritual of the native Tumbawa tribe. We trekked three months across the barren wasteland on elephant just to find that the Tumbawas had left five days earlier to study hotel management in Cairo.

By this time, we had exhausted our food supply and our elephant had slimmed to a svelte 90 pounds. We eventually ran out of clean underwear and Green started to get mean. Green got really mean.

We ran across a USO troop that had been left ⸻ mountain lake in WWII. Green started to play ⸻ expense. He charged them $5 each. First, he told ⸻ Hope had been mistaken for meat loaf and devoure⸻ in Alsace-Lorraine. Then he challenged them all ⸻ Trivial Pursuit. The poor sots didn't stand a chanc⸻ Baby Boomer edition.

Just then, a strange cry split the silence over the ⸻ warned Bruce, their lead dancer. "It might be those ⸻ mies!" Our hearts pounded in our throats. Suddenl⸻ filled with the patter of little feet, and over the mounta⸻

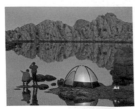

Chapter 5

Love comes at inappropriate times. Sometimes when you're too busy for it, sometimes when you want it least. Sometimes love comes when you're just not ready for it. Like last November when I finally coaxed Kitty Starlight to my hotel room only to find I had misplaced my handcuffs.

But Heather. I was ready for Heather. Blond, beautiful Heather. Magnetic, adventurous Heather. I met her in San Francisco, lunching at Swann's Oyster Bar. I had just finished a shoot for the latest contender to the hi-tech throne. She had just finished her fifth plate of sushi.

I asked if I might join her. "We are all joined together in the human chain of bondage," she replied. I sat down anyway.

Oh, the exhilaration of that first afternoon. We talked of our lives, our loves, our futures. Heather was a freelance philosopher. She didn't make much of an income, but her overhead was extremely reasonable. She had traveled the world over, and as she spoke of her adventures, I could picture our future together: running the bulls in Pamplona, perusing the ruins of the Incas, exploring the coral reefs of Bora Bora.

Suddenly, I realized I could not leave San Francisco without her. "Heather, I want you to..." My words were drowned by a deafening crash! Flames engulfed the restaurant, and Heather

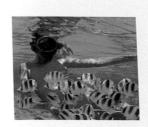

F Y I

October 7, 1985

A.
Sam Angeloff
S
Telephone:
(206)
Office 587-5393
(206)
Home 722-4428

AND
Writing Editing
and Communications
SERVICES
Consulting

For Progressive
Businesses
ASTUTE
VISIONARY
FARSIGHTED
INTERESTING
QUALITY

THIRD FLOOR,
NUMBER 323
Take outside
stairway to
third floor,
Room 323
1201
1239 First Ave. S.
Seattle, WA 98134
(SAME OFFICE,
NEW NUMBERING)

Just off the presses # 1:

In one form or another, Laird, Norton Trust Company has
served as an in-house financial institution for the Laird
and Norton timber families for more than 100 years.

The objective for this piece was to announce that the
trust business had been expanded to include wealthy folks
from outside the family, while preserving the firm's
rubbed woodgrain and old leather image.

I was chosen to write and manage the brochure. The
client selected Rick Eiber (from among several nominees)
for the design. Photographs were pickups from the Laird
Norton and Weyerhaeuser files.

Just off the presses # 2:

In 1982 I wrote a modest brochure for the law firm of
Reed McClure Moceri & Thonn. By mid-1985 they needed a
more elegant version (reflecting their new rents at
Columbia Center, and a new, longer name), and they
invited me back. The subdued design is by Mike Pfifer.

Regrettably, copies of this piece are in short supply,
and I can only send a photocopied sample of the opening
text. If you'd like to see the whole thing, I'll be glad
to bring you my portfolio copy.

Just off the presses # 3:

This mailing also introduces my long-awaited (much-
overdue, say some) stationery. I was perfectly happy
with my elderly Stationery House $69.50 Econo-Special,
but many of you had begun to complain.

Credits: Concept by Angeloff and Rick Eiber; lunch by
Lucianno. Text by Angeloff. Design and text counseling
by Eiber. Type by Type Gallery. Printing by Artcraft.
And many, many perforations by the Bayless Bindery.

A brief Commercial: Summer is over, and I'm back at the
keyboard, ready to do Big Things. Don't hesitate to call.
There's a lot of this stationery yet to be paid for.

Sam A. Angeloff

When writer Sam Angeloff took designer Rick Eiber to lunch to discuss his stationery package, they found themselves spending most of the meeting scratching over and editing each other's ideas. It was from this joint effort that the look of Angeloff's entire stationery system came. The letterhead and business card feature a perforated flap with address and telephone information covered with red editing marks. When the flap is folded back, the corrected information appears. The flap can be torn off or left in place. The flap on the note paper reads "Rough Draft."

When Angeloff wants to draw attention to a paragraph, he prints the information on the letterhead using the "red pencil" style of the stationery. Additionally, every five to six months Angeloff sends out samples of his better projects to existing clients with a cover letter.

Because Angeloff uses his stationery for promotion as well as everyday business, he has been able to create a strong image for his firm.

Audience: Corporate, advertising agencies and design firms
Description: Two-color, perforated letterhead, business cards, and note paper.

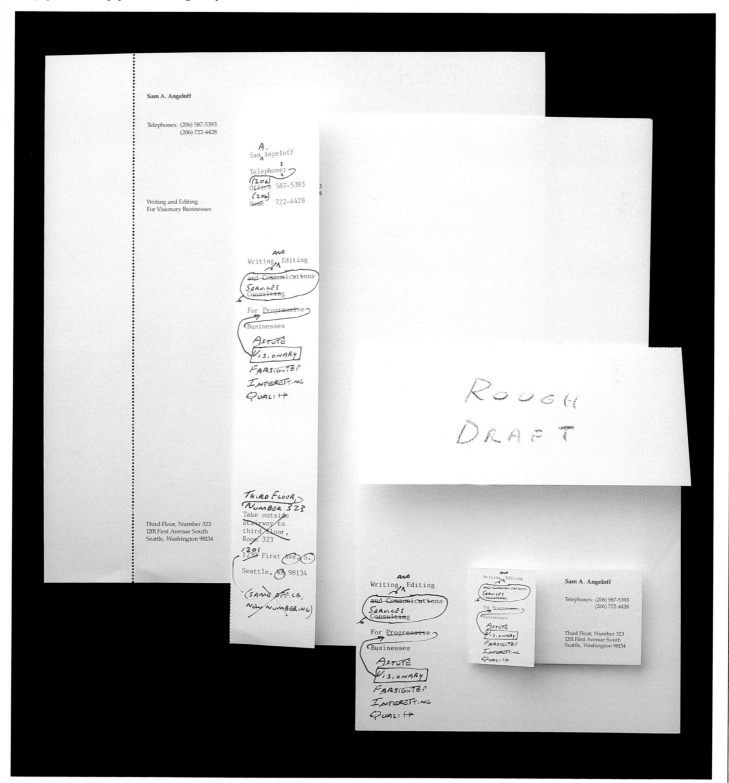

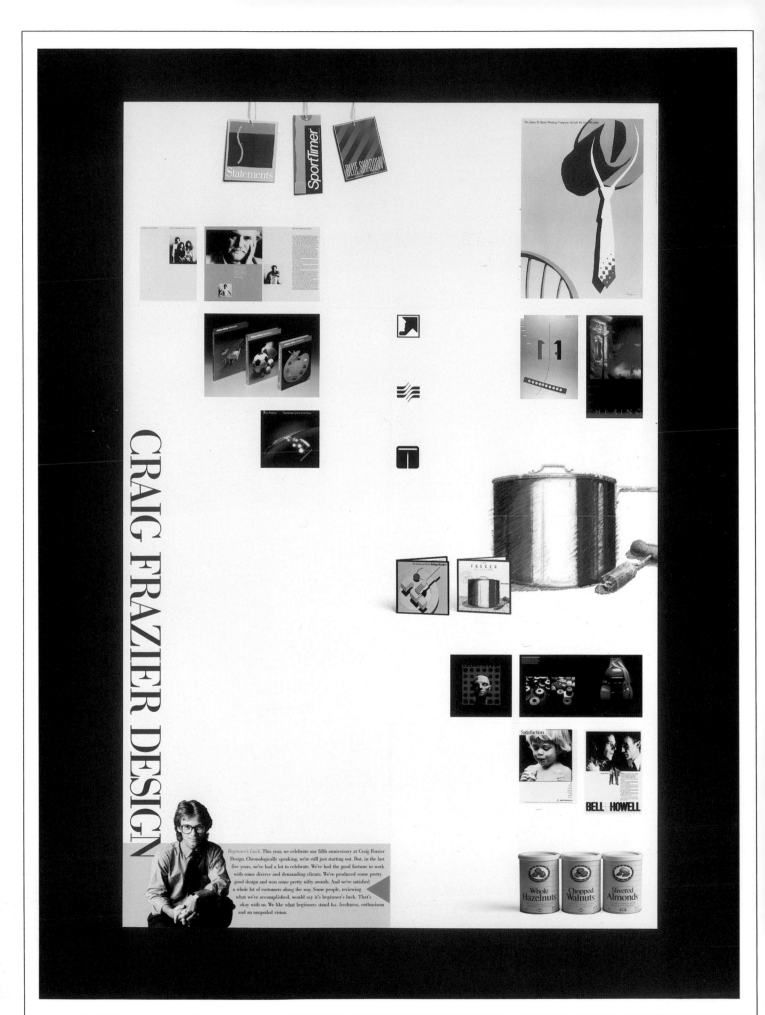

CRAIG FRAZIER DESIGN

Beginner's Luck. This year, we celebrate our fifth anniversary at Craig Frazier Design. Chronologically speaking, we're still just starting out. But, in the last five years, we've had a lot to celebrate. We've had the good fortune to work with some diverse and demanding clients. We've produced some pretty good design and won some pretty nifty awards. And we've satisfied a whole lot of customers along the way. Some people, reviewing what we've accomplished, would say it's beginner's luck. That's okay with us. We like what beginners stand for: freshness, enthusiasm and an unspoiled vision.

Craig Frazier Design

The direct mail piece for Craig Frazier Design was a conscious effort to establish a look for the studio while at the same time making a strong impression on prospective clients. "I wanted people to look at this, and see all the work on one page, and think, 'These guys are tremendously versatile.'" The poster shows fifteen projects along with a portrait of Craig and a statement about the firm. On a separate sheet is a diagram of the poster with captions for each project.

One very strong element of the poster is the photograph of Craig Frazier. The portrait introduced Craig to prospective clients and eventually, it became an identifying image for the firm.

Audience: *Corporate*
Description: *22" x 34" poster and 8½" x 11" fact sheet with envelope*
Quantity: *1,500*

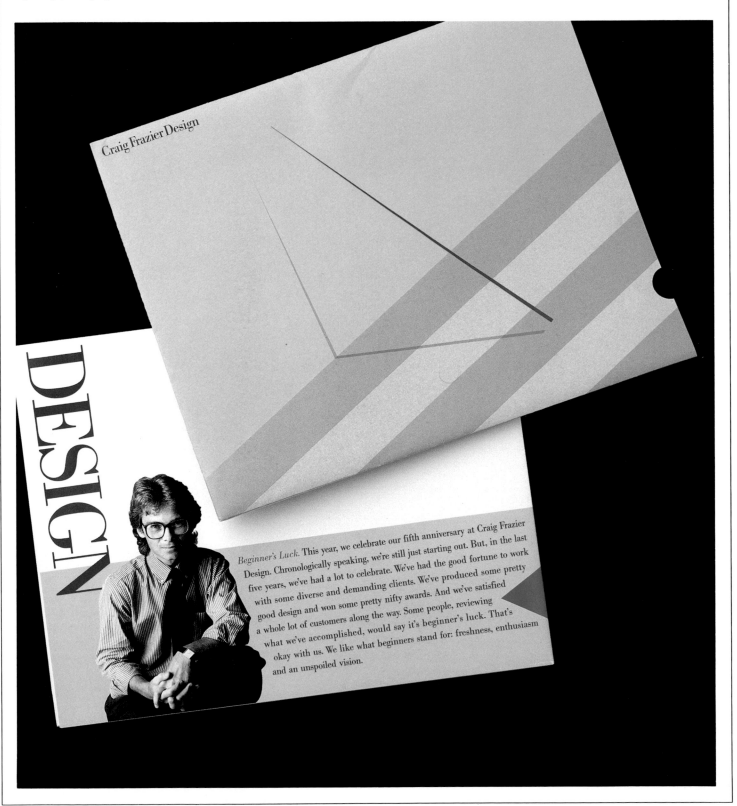

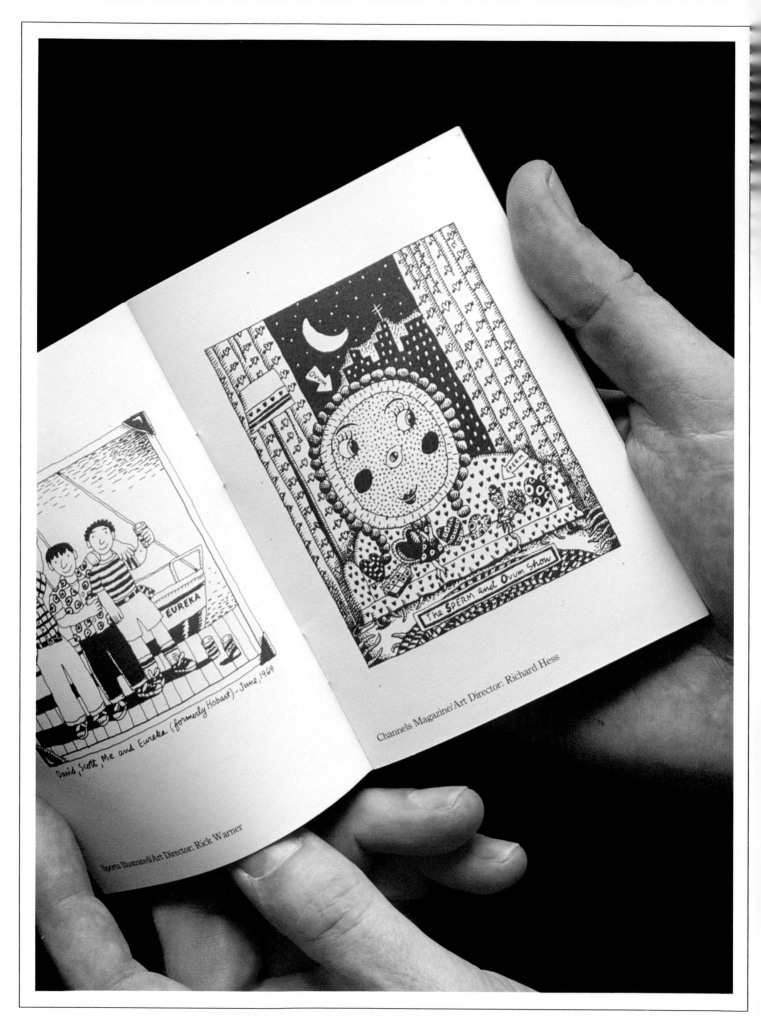

David, Scott, Me and Eureka (formerly Hobart) – June, 1969

Sports Illustrated/Art Director: Rick Warner

The SPERM and OVUM show

Channels Magazine/Art Director: Richard Hess

PUTTING TOGETHER A COMPELLING PORTFOLIO

The backbone of any self-promotion strategy is the "portfolio" piece. Few creatives have the time to visit every potential client, and many potential clients don't have the time to see us. How we present our work to these people can determine whether or not they *ever* will take the time to see us.

Beyond being a "creative" presentation, it is important that the portfolio piece presents your work in a format that will make the work look its best, and in a format that will be understood by the prospect. For instance, people who are responsible for buying advertising photography may respond to a poster, while someone buying annual report photography would rather see the work in a smaller format.

Here are some questions to ask yourself:

Who is the audience?

Is there more than one audience?

What form will these audiences respond to?

What form will allow additions or deletions? Is this necessary?

Does the portfolio need to be added to? Updated? Should it be flexible for updating?

Should it be flexible for customized presentations?

How long will the piece be useful before it becomes dated?

How much work should be shown?

How old can the work be and still show it?

Should the portfolio be specialized? Only trademarks, for instance?

Will the work shown lead to more like work? In other words, am I showing a sample because I like it or because I think that it will influence a potential client? Along this same line, will my peers be more impressed or the potential client?

Does the budget exist to make the work look "good?"

Along with the samples, what else will a client want to know?

Should a client list be included?

Background information on the principals or staff?

Should the office or studio be shown?

Should there be photos of the principals or staff? (Will this make the piece go out of date if anyone leaves the firm?)

Should awards be listed? (Be careful with this one. A corporate vice president may care a great deal that you have an award for the bank best annual report three years ago, while an agency art director may have no interest at all in such an award.)

The questions are to help you establish your own priorities. Keep in mind that no piece can be all things to all people.

Simms Taback
Facing page: The black & white illustrations of Simms Taback are reproduced in a small brochure which was distributed by Simms and his rep to a national advertising and editorial audience. Credit is given to the art director or client of each drawing, a subtle way of giving a client list.
Audience: *Advertising, editorial, and corporate*
Description: *16 page, 3½" x 5" brochure*
Quantity: *4,000*

Barrie Rokeach Photography
Photographer Barrie Rokeach sends out a direct mail package that resembles a film processing envelope. Inside the envelope is a 35mm film cassette. When the film is pulled from the cassette, Barrie's portfolio is revealed on the film.
Audience: *Corporate and advertising*
Description: *Film cassette with film strip in envelope*
Quantity: *1,000*

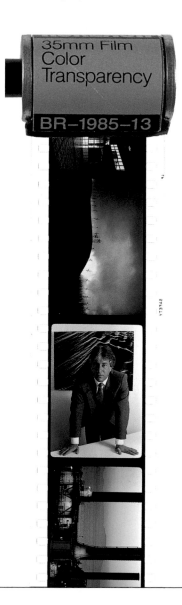

James Lienhart Design

Chicago designer Jim Lienhart's trademark brochure has for its cover Jim's own distinctive logo. The 90-page brochure features one mark per page, all printed in a purple ink.

"I've had good reaction over the years to the brochure, but what people relate to the most is the opening copy," states Jim.

Here is part of the opening page copy:

"What makes a great trademark? I don't know. But if I see one, I know it. To me you have to feel the nature of the company. The CBS eye, the woolmark, and the trademark for Continental Airlines are examples of what I mean. Once you understand all of the marketing aspects of the company,

and you are aware of the politics involved, and you know the range of applications for the many different audiences, then you're about halfway there.

"I've had some great clients and a few turkeys, but the challenge to produce that special identity remains exciting and rewarding."

Audience: *Corporate*
Description: *5" x 11", 90-page wiro-bound brochure*
Quantity: *1,500*

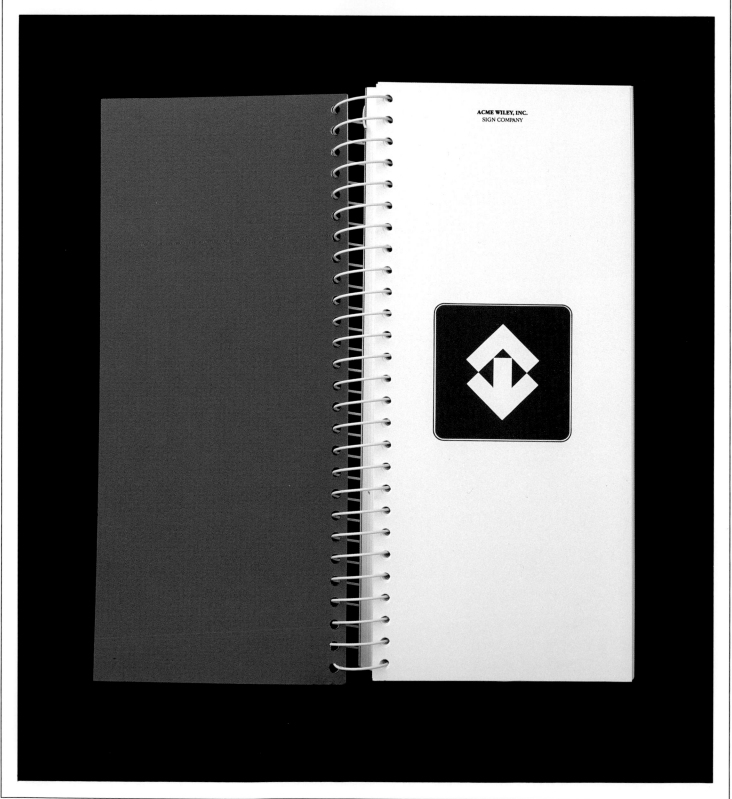

**Richards, Brock, Miller,
Mitchell & Associates**

*The trademarks designed by RBMM in Dallas
are displayed in a series of small brochures begun
in 1970. The brochures, which all follow the
same format, feature captions that explain the
purpose of the individual marks in short, lively
sentences. The brochures utilize colorful covers
to distinguish the different issues, while inside
the colors have remained gray and black.*

Audience: *Corporate*
Description: *Five 4" x 9", 16-page brochures*
Quantity: *2,000 apiece*

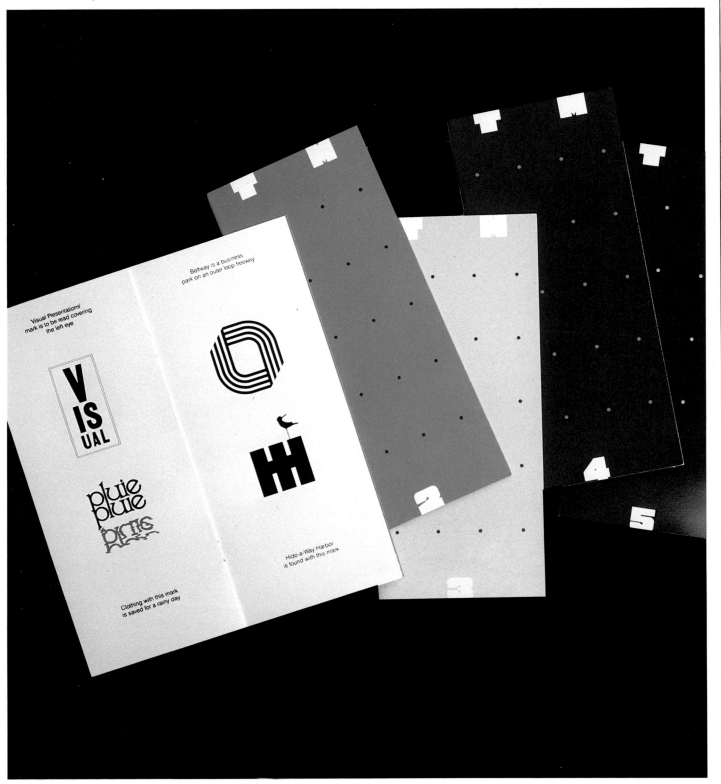

Ron Scott Photography
One of the longer-running success stories, the handmade portfolios of Houston photographer Ron Scott
have been showing up in design firms and advertising
agencies for over fifteen years. Ron's original idea has
held up over time because he constantly updates the
images that make up his sample booklets.

The samplers are comprised of photographic prints
Ron makes in his own studio. He trims and binds the
prints together with a film negative for a cover.

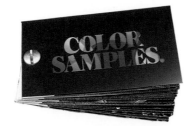

The title "Color Samples" plays off the well-known
ink sample booklets of the same form that art directors
and designers are familiar with.
Audience: *Art directors and designers*
Description: *Individual 2" x 4" photographic prints
postbound*
Quantity: *Varies*

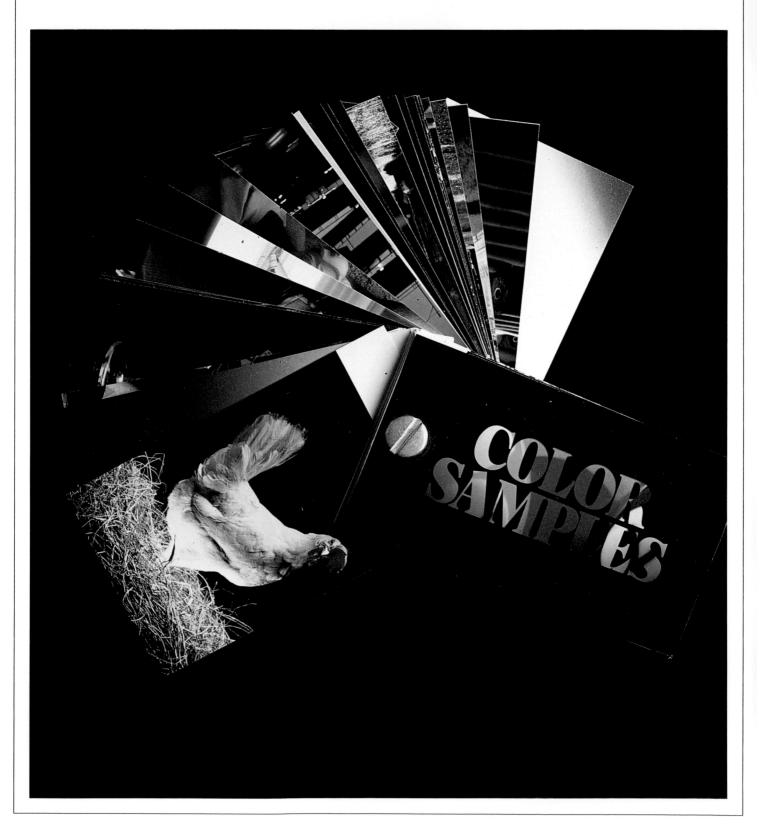

Hans Staartjes Photography

The self-promotion mailer of Hans Staartjes Photography was a direct response to a major problem. "Nobody knew who I was," states Hans. "After coming to this country and working in a portrait studio for three years, people didn't really know who I was when I went out on my own."

The mailer Hans sent out is a collection of six photographs, only two of which had been previously published. An important part of the package is a cover sheet which tells about Staartjes's background.

Hans believes the success of the piece, in part, is because of the personal nature of some of the work. "I was absolutely baffled that it worked so well. I have received many comments from other photographers and one real solid client so

far. I now am going to follow up with another piece, probably with even more personal work."

Audience: *Art directors and designers*
Description: *Nine four-color sheets, 8" x 8", postbound*
Quantity: *500*

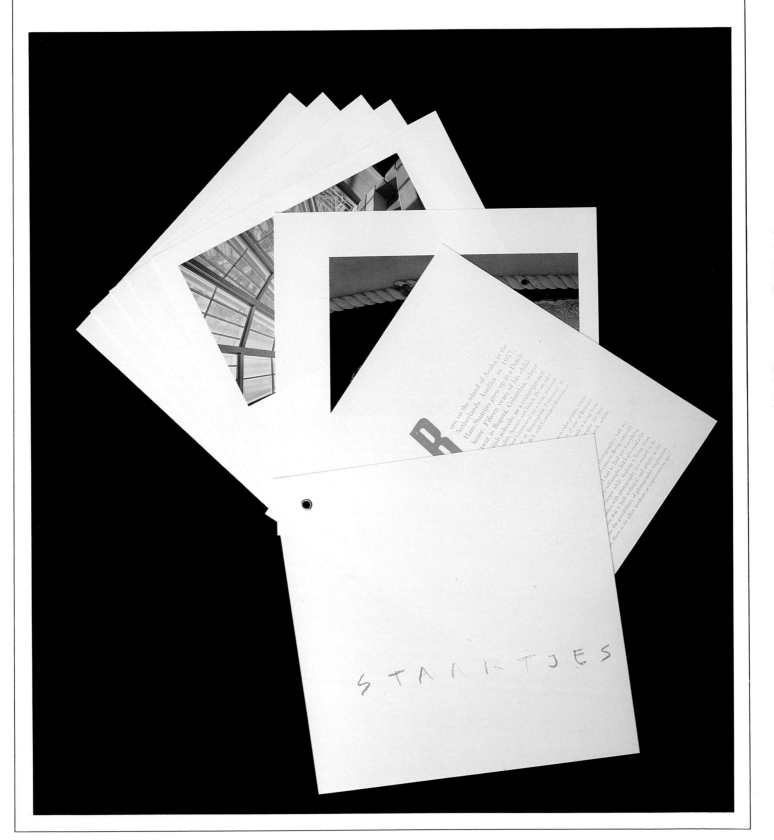

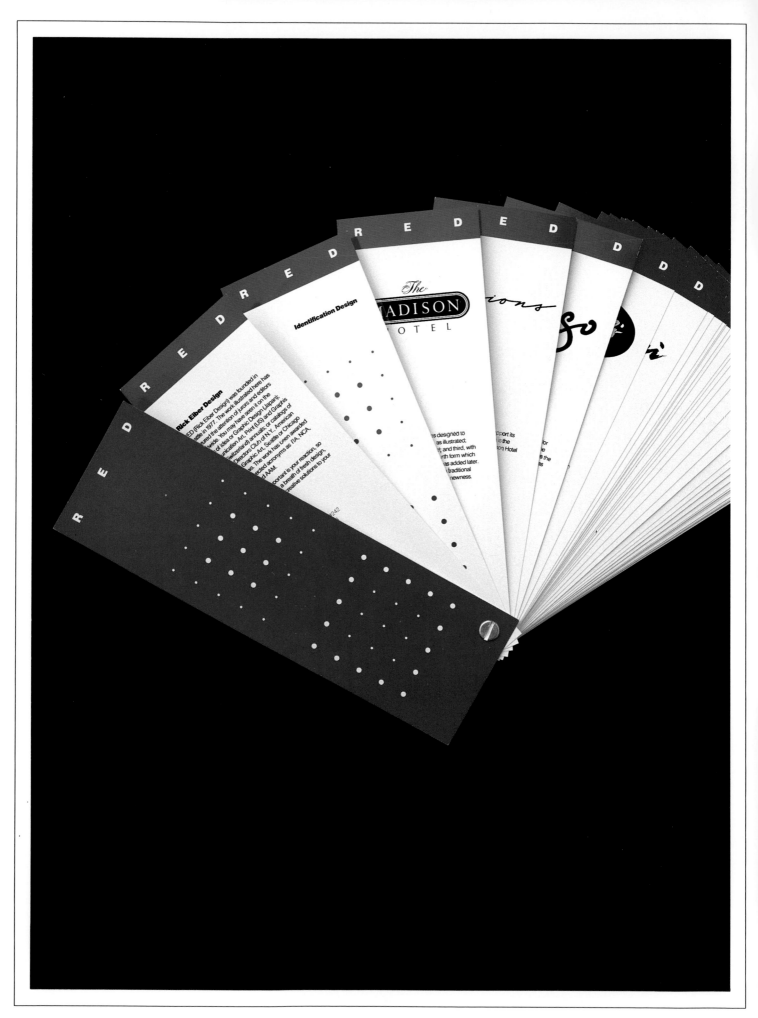

Rick Elber Design

RED (Rick Elber Design) was founded in Seattle in 1977. The work illustrated here has featured the attention of jurors and editors worldwide. You may have seen it on the pages of Idea or Graphic Design (Japan); Communication Art, Print (US) and Graphis (Switzerland) annuals; or catalogs of Art Directors Club of N.Y., American Graphic Art, Seattle or Chicago shows. The work has been awarded gold and silver acronyms as PA, NCA, and AAM.

...portant is your reaction, so ...a breath of fresh design, ...creative solutions to your

Identification Design

...s designed to ...as illustrated; ...t and third, with ...rth form which ...as added later. ...n traditional ...newness.

...pport its
...s the
...ison Hotel

Rick Eiber Design

Rick Eiber plays off the visual implication of the firm's initials, RED, to create an umbrella concept for all his marketing materials. The firm's logos and collateral samples are presented in a manner similar to a color swatch book, with individual sheets postbound together. Across the tip of each sheet is a color bar with the initials RED.

Audience: *Corporate*
Description: *46 sheets, 2³⁄₄" x 8¹⁄₂", postbound*
Quantity: *500*

HIXO

The HIXO Sampler is made up of individual sheets of trademarks that can be assembled in various arrangements. "This was never a mail-out campaign. We make up the presentations as needed," states Mike Hicks. "We printed all the sheets at once and keep them loose here at the office. If we are pitching a restaurant, we may only show restaurant logos. Or we might pitch a bank and put the bank logos up front. Obviously we can add to the collection of logos at any time."

Audience: *Corporate and advertising*
Description: *3¹⁄₂" x 3¹⁄₂" sheets, postbound*
Quantity: *Various*

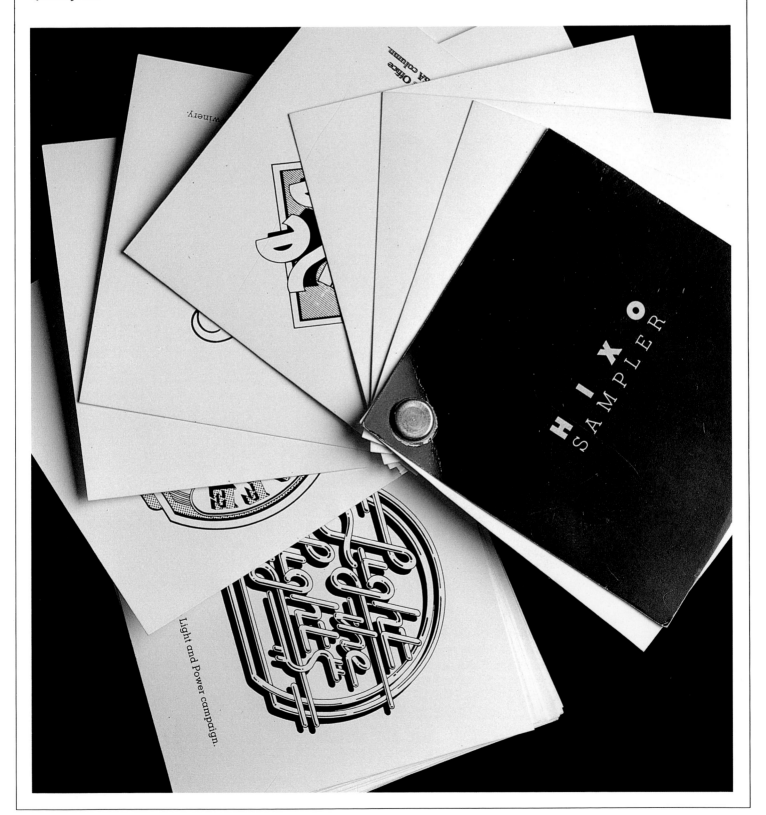

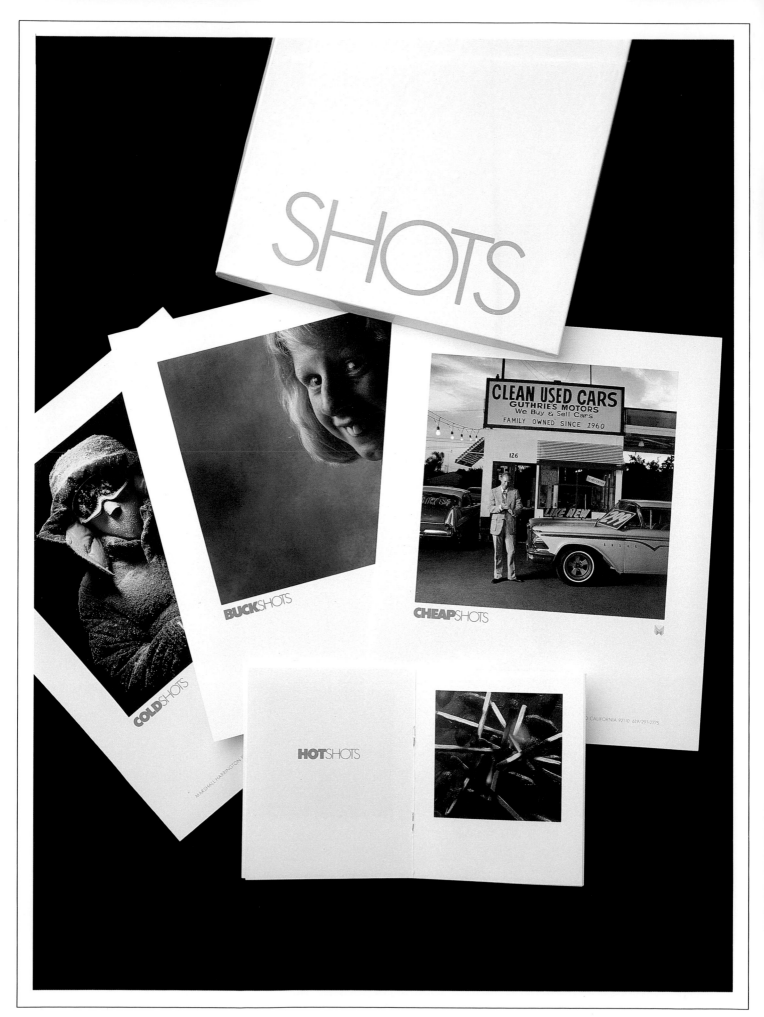

Marshall Harrington Photography

Photographer Marshall Harrington's promotion is labeled "Shots." Hot Shots, Long Shots, Cheap Shots, Big Shots. Marshall worked with art director John Vitro to come up with this concept, then took specific photographs to illustrate the individual "shots." The result is a boxed set of ten sheets that make one type of presentation, and a small brochure with the

same photographs that can be used as a mailer.
Audience: *Advertising and corporate*
Description: *Box with 8" x 10" inserts and 4" x 5", 20-page brochure*
Quantity: *2,000*

Steve Brady Photography

The boxed set of prints that Steve Brady uses began as an initial mailer with 16 individual sheets. Later 12 more sheets were printed and mailed out with a fly sheet with the cover line, "Brady thrives in all kinds of light."

"I mailed the second set out to the people that received the first set," says Brady. "I can combine the sets when responding to an inquiry."
Audience: *Corporate, advertising agencies and design firms*
Description: *8½" x 11" sheets, boxed*
Quantity: *500*

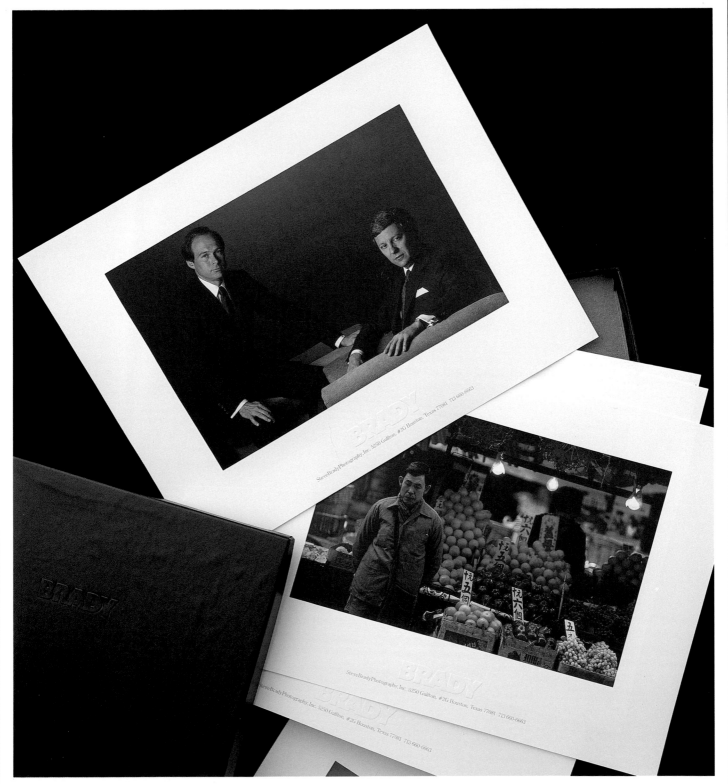

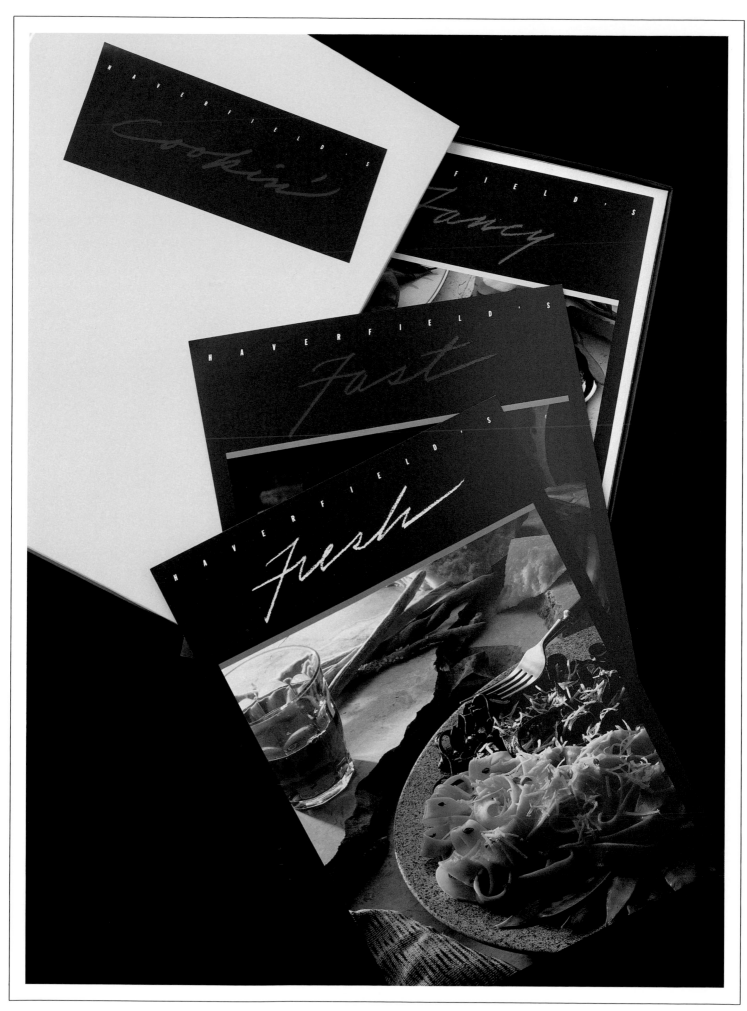

Pat Haverfield Photography

After working with another firm for seven years, Dallas-based photographer Pat Haverfield needed name identification when he launched his business. Working with a home economist, a stylist, a designer, a writer, and a rep, Pat produced a boxed portfolio targeted at the specialized food industry. The portfolio consists of individual sheets with a photograph specifically taken to illustrate a cover line, such as "Fast," "Fancy," or "Fresh." On the back of

each sheet is a copy block that starts out with a play on the same words, such as "Haverfield's Fast."

Audience: *Food industry ad agencies and design firms*
Description: *8″ x 11½″ box with label, six inserts.*
Quantity: *950*

Dyer/Kahn

The Los Angeles design firm of Dyer/Kahn uses a pocket folder with inserts, allowing the firm to make customized presentations to its clients. The inserts can be updated, and each presentation can be customized with a cover letter and additional materials.
Audience: *Corporate*
Description: *9″ x 12″ six-panel pocket folder with inserts*
Quantity: *5,000*

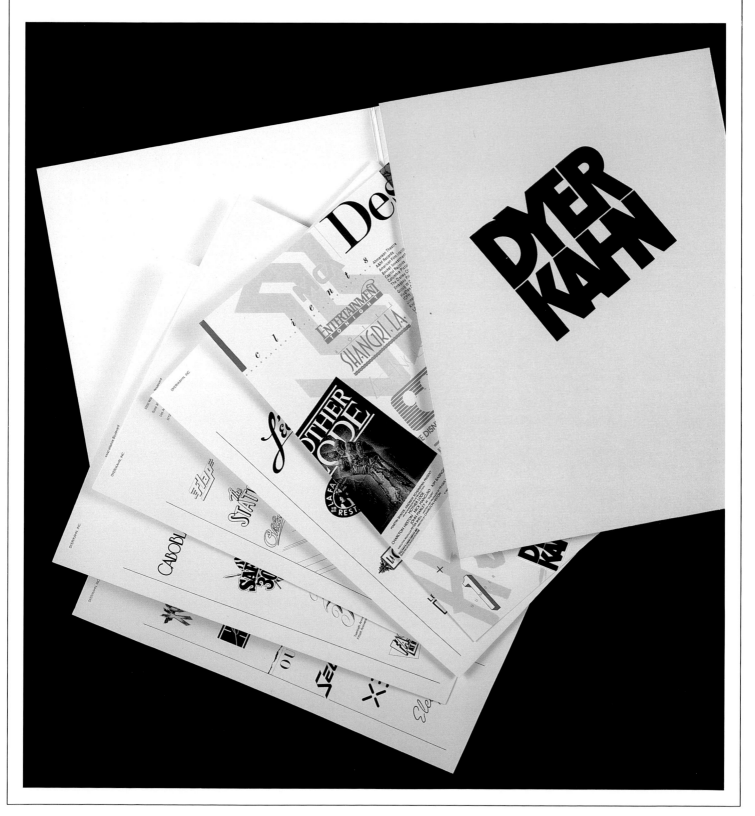

FASHION

PHOTO DIRECTION

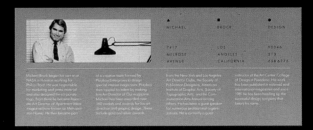

MICHAEL   BROCK   DESIGN

7417   LOS   90046
MELROSE   ANGELES,   213
AVENUE   CALIFORNIA   658 6775

Michael Brock began his career at NASA in Houston working for Philco/Ford. He was responsible for marketing and press material and also designed the corporate logos. From there he became Associate Art Director of Apartment Ideas magazine (now known as Metropolitan Home). He then became part of a creative team formed by Playboy Enterprises to design special interest magazines. Playboy then tapped his talent by making him Art Director of Oui magazine. Michael has been awarded over 160 medals and awards for his art direction and graphic design. These include gold and silver awards from the New York and Los Angeles Art Director Clubs, the Society of Publication Designers, American Institute of Graphic Arts, Society of Typographic Arts, and the Communication Arts Annual among others. He has been a guest speaker for numerous professional organizations. He is currently a guest instructor at the Art Center College of Design in Pasadena. His work has been published in national and international magazines and since 1981 he has been heading up the successful design company that bears his name.

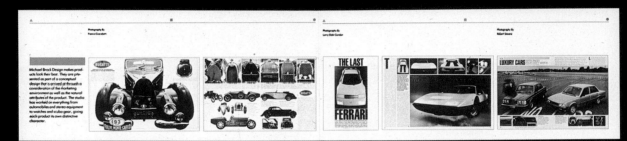

Michael Brock Design makes products look their best. They are presented as part of a conceptual design that is arrived at through a consideration of the marketing environment as well as the natural attributes of the product. The studio has worked on everything from automobiles and stereo equipment to watches and scuba gear, giving each product its own distinctive character.

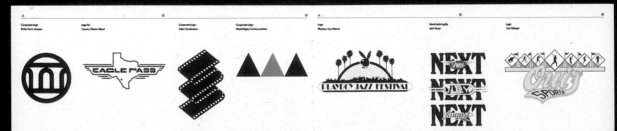

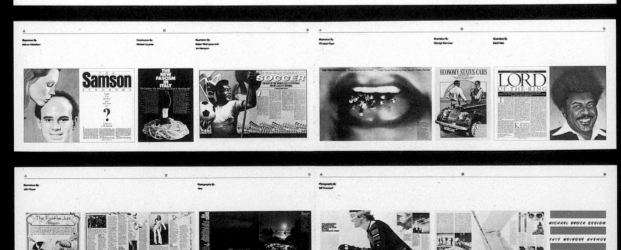

Michael Brock Design

After a long tenure as an art director for a national magazine, Michael Brock needed a portfolio to send out that was more than just magazine spreads. Incorporating his freelance work with the magazine work, Michael put together a portfolio that was divided up by themes: Art Direction, Editorial Design, Photo Direction, Graphic Design, Fashion, Products.

"I knew that I needed to tell people that I could do more than art direct a magazine, so I broke it down into the various aspects of what I had been doing. Basically, most of the work I

was showing was from the magazine. But I presented it in such a way to show I could handle any area of design."

Audience: *Advertising agencies, publishing companies, and corporate*
Description: *Six 9" x 4" brochures with insert, boxed*
Quantity: *1,000*

Chuck Burggraf Photography

Photographer Chuck Burggraf had built up a reputation in the Denver area for good table top photography, but he wanted to expand into other areas. The promotion package that Burggraf produced is a series of eight sheets featuring location and "graphic style" photographs that can be mailed individually or included with cover sheets in a handsome portfolio folder.

Audience: *Art directors and designers*
Description: *5" x 7" sheets in folder*
Quantity: *1,000*

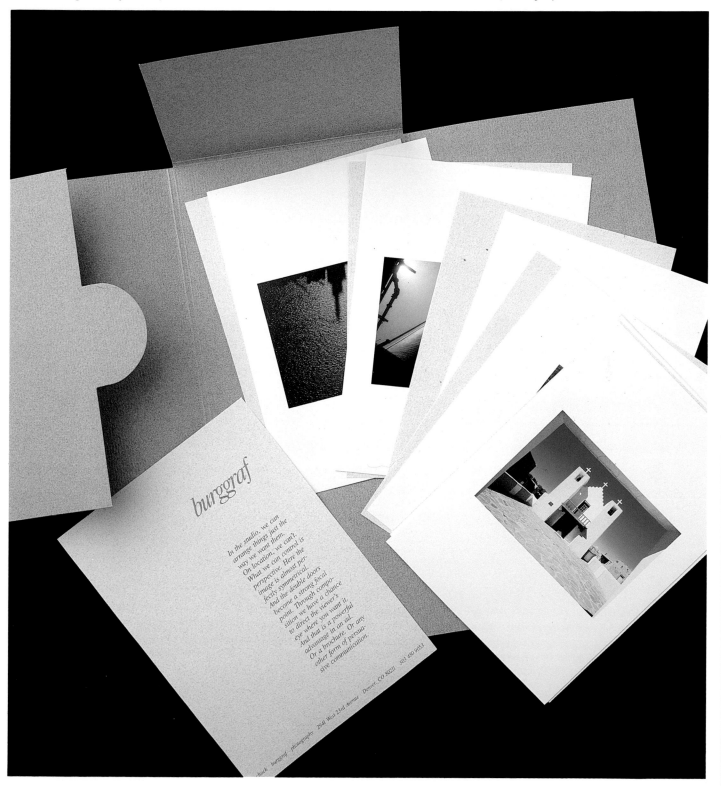

Chermayeff & Geismar Associates
The large New York design firm of Chermayeff & Geismar Associates has produced specialized promotional efforts for its services, two of which are shown on this spread.

To present the firm's environmental work, a brushed aluminum folder titled "Chermayeff & Geismar Associates, Art in Architecture" is used as a carrier for photo prints of specific projects. The prints each feature one photo, with a credit line that describes the work (such as "sculpture"

or "mural"), the client, the location, and the architect. The presentation can be customized for a particular client with additional prints on a specific project.
Audience: *Corporate and architecture*
Description: *Aluminum folder with paper pocket, photographic print inserts*
Quantity: *Various*

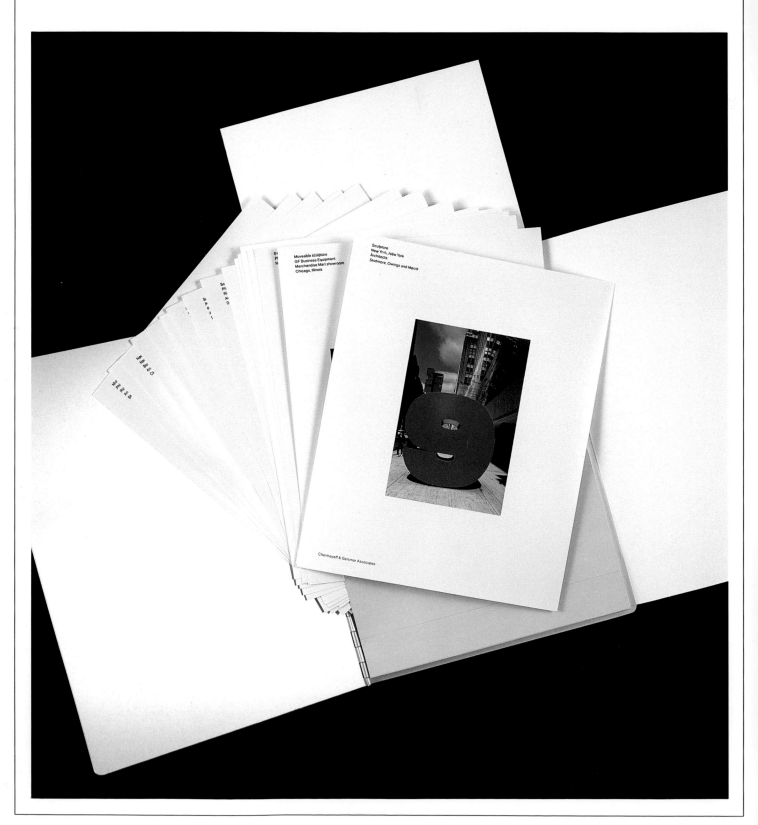

Chermayeff & Geismar Associates
*The trademark business of Chermayeff &
Geismar Associates is promoted in a large-scale,
100-page monograph. The wiro-bound presen-
tation features large marks with applications.
The book is indexed and lists the present and
past members of the firm.*
Audience: *Corporate*
Description: *9" x 12", 100-page wiro-
bound book*
Quantity: *500*

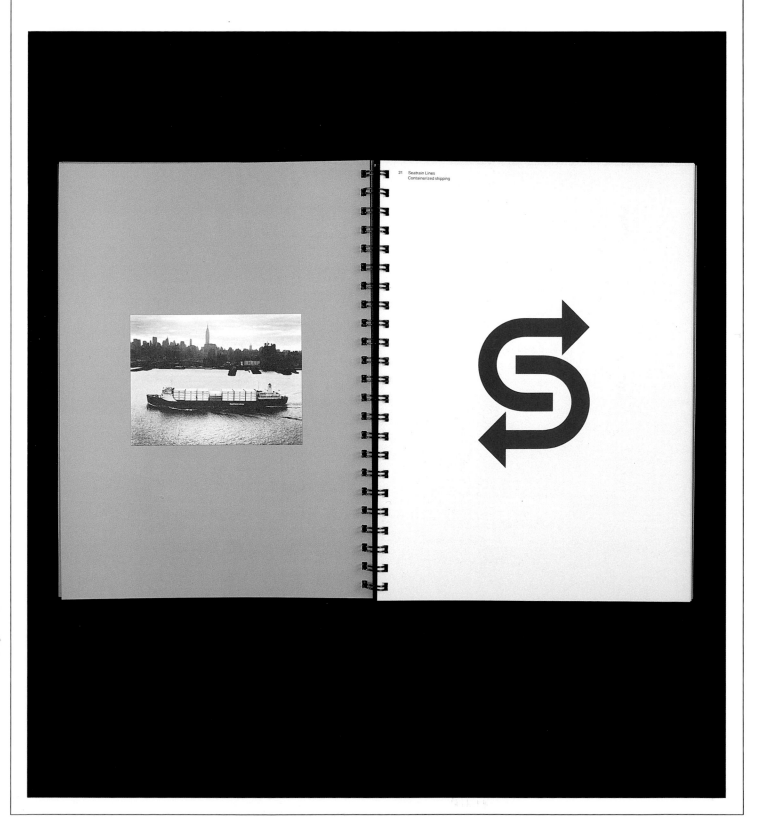

21   Seatrain Lines
     Containerized shipping

Cross Associates

The imposing brochure of Cross Associates, the California-based design firm, is organized by sections. The company's philosophy, the key personnel, the portfolio, the client makeup and the accounting procedures are all given plenty of space. Although the brochure features many pages of four-color samples of its work, the spread that gets the most attention is of the forms.

"It's funny," says Jim Cross, "but that spread always does make the client stop and look. I guess it's because it is a world they understand. They want to know that the project will be done in an orderly way, and that they will be kept informed. The forms say, 'We know what your concerns are.'"

Audience: *Corporate*
Description: *11" x 12½", 72-page perfect-bound brochure*
Quantity: *1,000*

Lowell Williams Design

The hard-cover corporate brochure of Lowell Williams Design features many spreads that show the work in composed, studio photographs. The effect of the presentation is to give a greater feeling of depth to the spreads, many of which play off a studio photograph against a flat representation of a brochure.

Audience: *Corporate*
Description: *8" x 12", 66-page hard-bound brochure*
Quantity: *1,000*

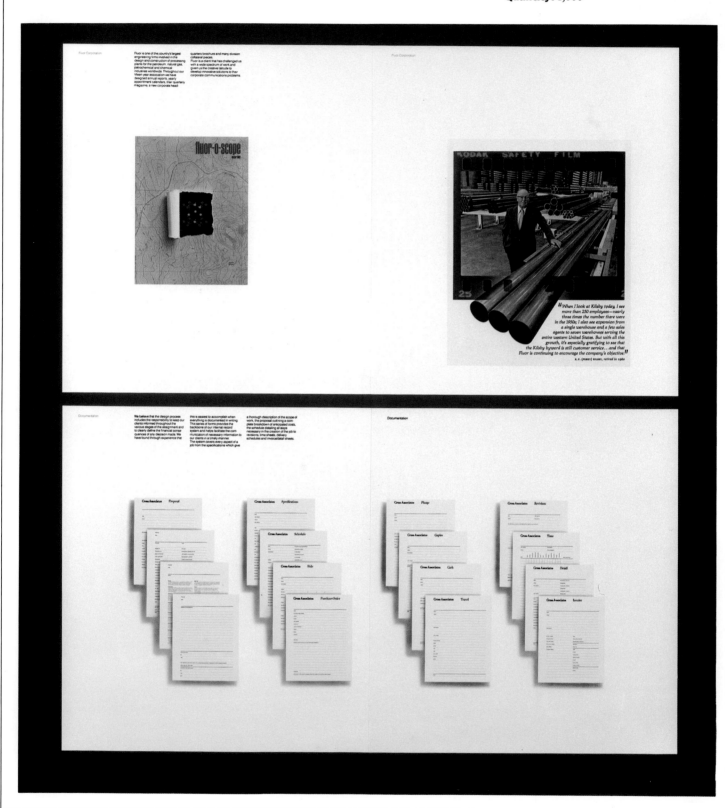

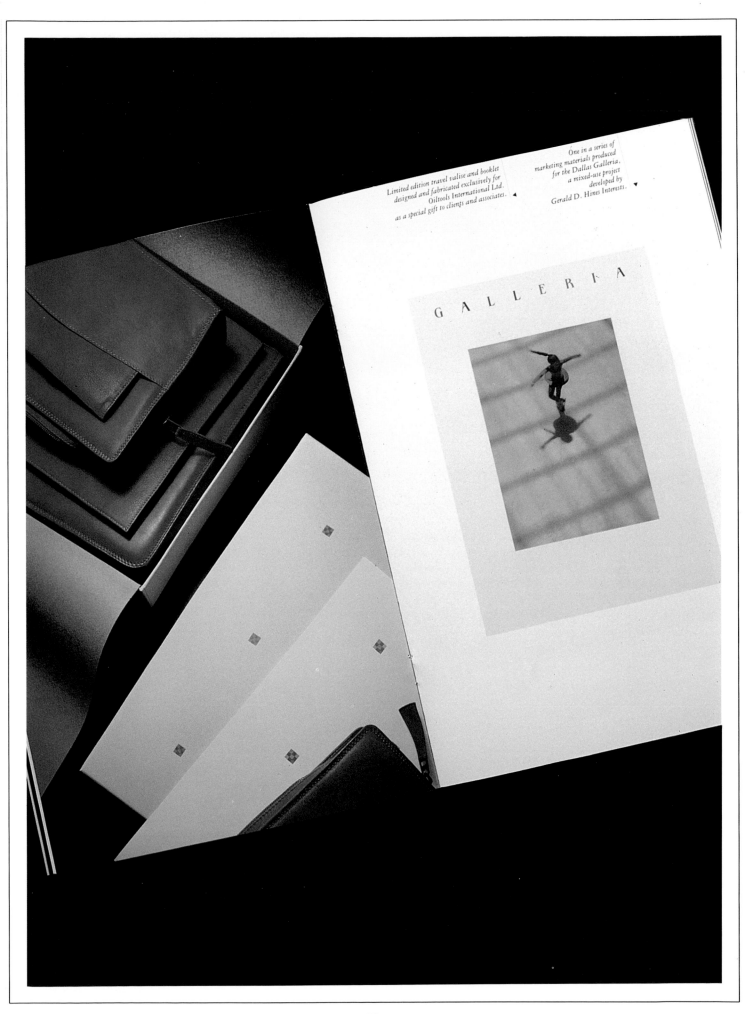

Limited edition travel valise and booklet designed and fabricated exclusively for Oiltools International Ltd. as a special gift to clients and associates. ◀

One in a series of marketing materials produced for the Dallas Galleria, a mixed-use project developed by Gerald D. Hines Interests. ◀

GALLERIA

The Graphic Expression, Inc.

The brochure for The Graphic Expression resembles an annual report for a major corporation, without the financials. After an introductory statement on parchment (with the interior of the design firm seen through the paper), the brochure displays the work of their major clients. Besides the work, their clients are shown and quoted.

Audience: *Corporate*

Description: *8″ x 11½″ full-color, 36-page brochure*

Quantity: *3,000*

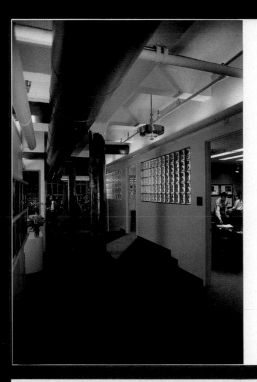

. . . it reflects on the experiences of companies which are leaders in their industries, led by people with foresight and imagination.

What links them together is a recognition of the role of superior communications design as a means of conveying corporate success and leadership.

In the following sections, you will encounter successful companies–investment banks, retail organizations, high technology firms and automotive companies–which symbolize the best in American industry. Some have been part of the economic landscape seemingly forever. Others arrived only a few years ago on the forefront of the technological and service booms.

You will encounter examples of how they use superior design in the form of annual reports, capabilities brochures, marketing literature and other publications to communicate their leadership positions.

You will also encounter some of the thoughts of professionals whose ability to think creatively–and often courageously–helps convey the strengths of their companies.

But to begin this book, you should first encounter the connective tissue in this process of conveying leadership through communications design, The Graphic Expression, Inc.

This book presents ideas, methods and work that have made The Graphic Expression a leader in communications design.

will accept nothing less than the best and that they are prepared to act competitively to find it.

The way First Boston meets this challenge is through aggressive marketing. The cornerstone of marketing is communications. Those who contribute most to our communications are the people at The Graphic Expression.

The Graphic Expression provides us with good graphics, clean, contemporary design and superior service–all essential to good marketing communications.

Perhaps most important, they think for us as though they were part of us. They act as truly part of the team, yet always with a critical degree of objectivity. From a communications standpoint, they sometimes understand us better than we understand ourselves."
Nancy Field

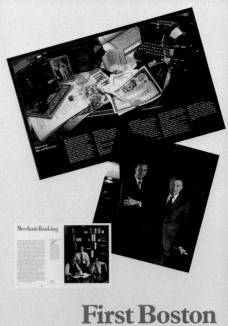

"Communications is the means of conveying the quality of an organization."

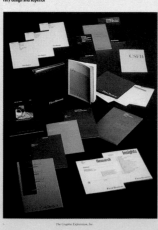

First Boston

Mason Morfit

The pages of Mason Morfit's brochure look a lot like a major corporation annual report. For good reason. A graphic designer turned photographer, Mason designed his brochure himself to appeal to the designer's sensitivities—designers who would use him for corporate photography. "Having been a designer, I'm often sent out on photographic shoots when the designer can't go along."

That was the first part of his strategy. The second was targeting his audience. Mason mailed half of the brochures to members of the nation's largest graphic design organization. The other half was mailed to a list made up of names from the "Fortune 500."

Audience: *Corporate and design firms*
Description: *32-page, 8½" x 11" brochure*
Quantity: *5,000*

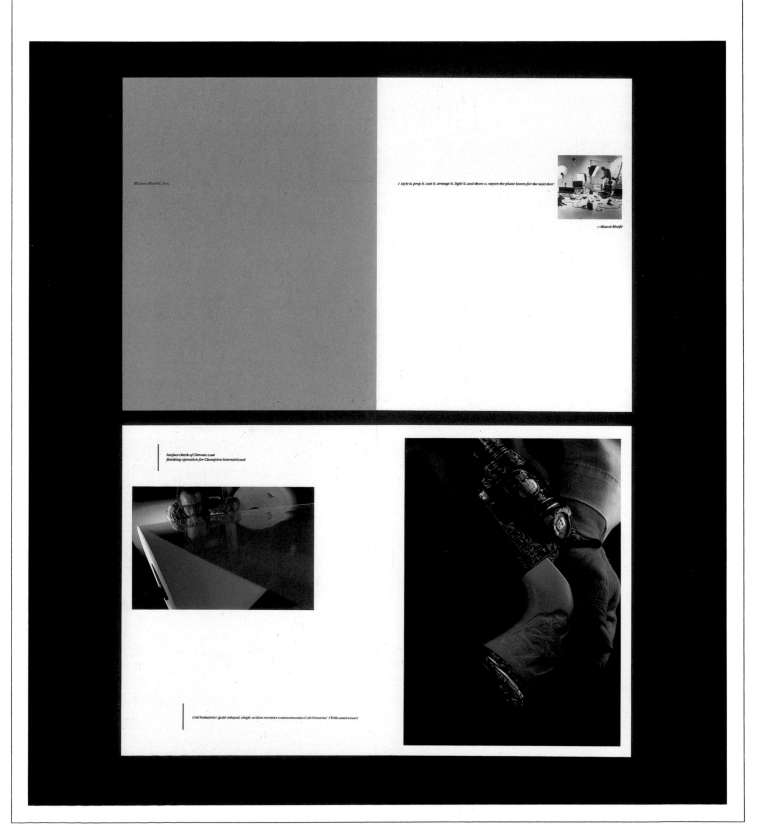

Gladstone Studio

Photographer Gary Gladstone's brochure designed by John Vogler is laid out to show his photography in a "corporate" setting. The brochure is very effective, with portraits juxtaposed to high tech detail photos. The perfect bound brochure has heavy, laminated covers. On the inside front and inside back covers, quotes endorsing Gary appear, with credits. The strength of the quotes are their sources, from corporations as well as magazines such as Fortune *and* Business Week.

Audience: *Corporate and design firms*

Description: *8¾" x 11¾", 36-page, perfect bound brochure*

Quantity: *2,000*

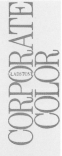

Hedrich-Blessing Photography

The Chicago photographic firm of Hedrich-Blessing, with eight photographers producing photographs, needed a brochure to sell the firm as well as the individuals. The design solution of Lowell Williams is a brochure that features the work of each individual photographer separated from another with fly-sheet dividers. All the photographs in the brochure are on coated paper, and all the divider pages and copy pages are on uncoated text paper.

Audience: *Corporate, advertising, and design firms*

Description: *7½" x 12", 72-page brochure*

Quantity: *2,500*

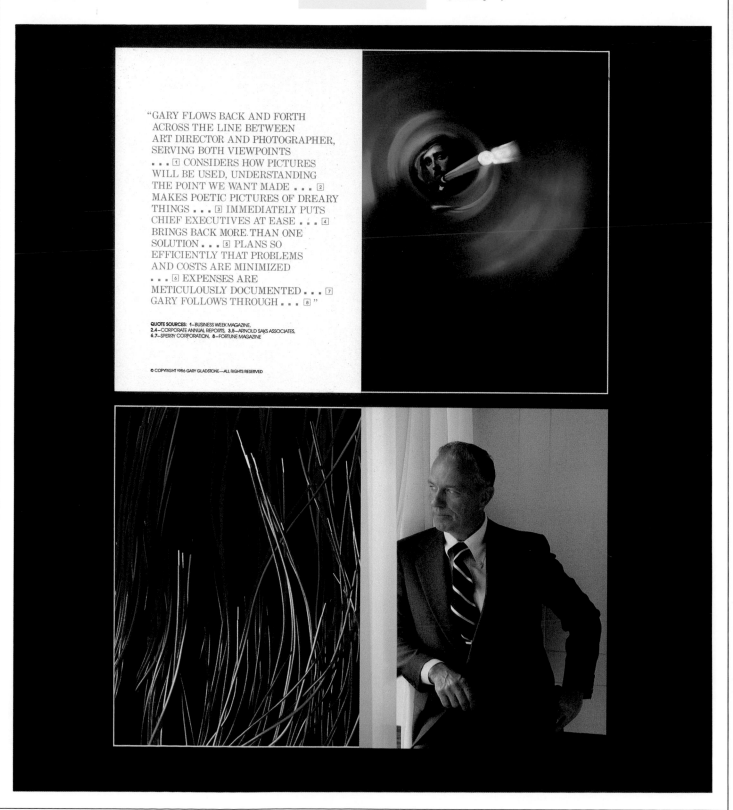

JIM HEDRICH

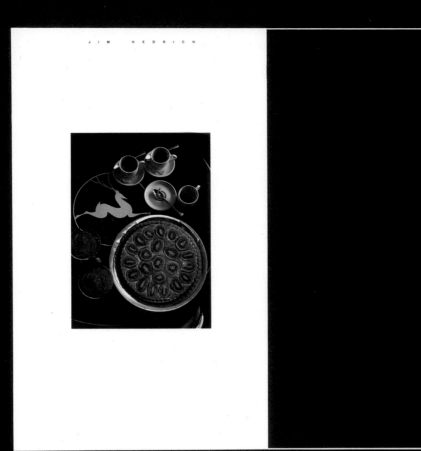

JON MILLER

JON MILLER

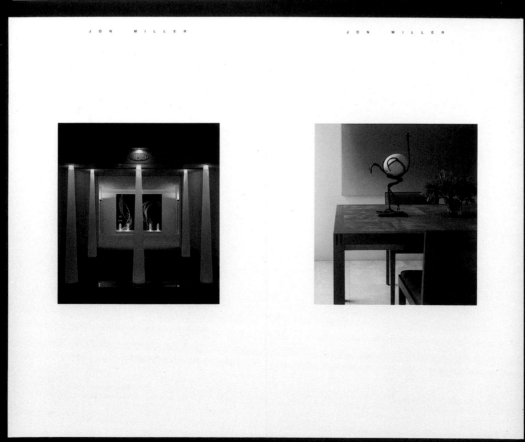

Pentagram Design

The annual review of Pentagram Design (London/ New York/San Francisco) is a look back at the projects and activities of the year. The 20-page annual goes into detail on a project by project basis.

Audience: *Clients, prospective clients, and friends*

Description: *8¼" x 11¾", 20-page booklet*

Quantity: *4,000*

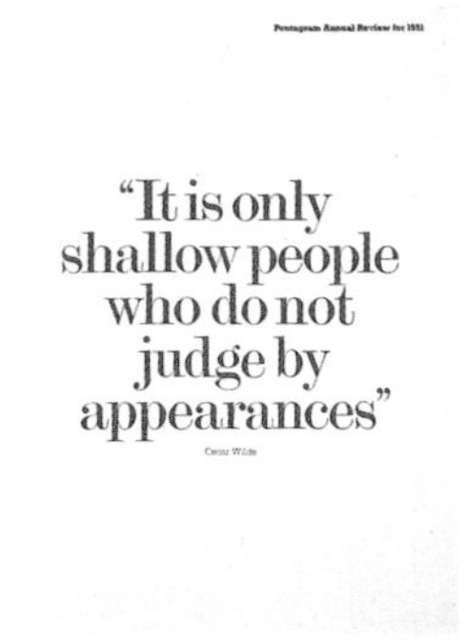

Pentagram Annual Review for 1981

"It is only shallow people who do not judge by appearances"

Oscar Wilde

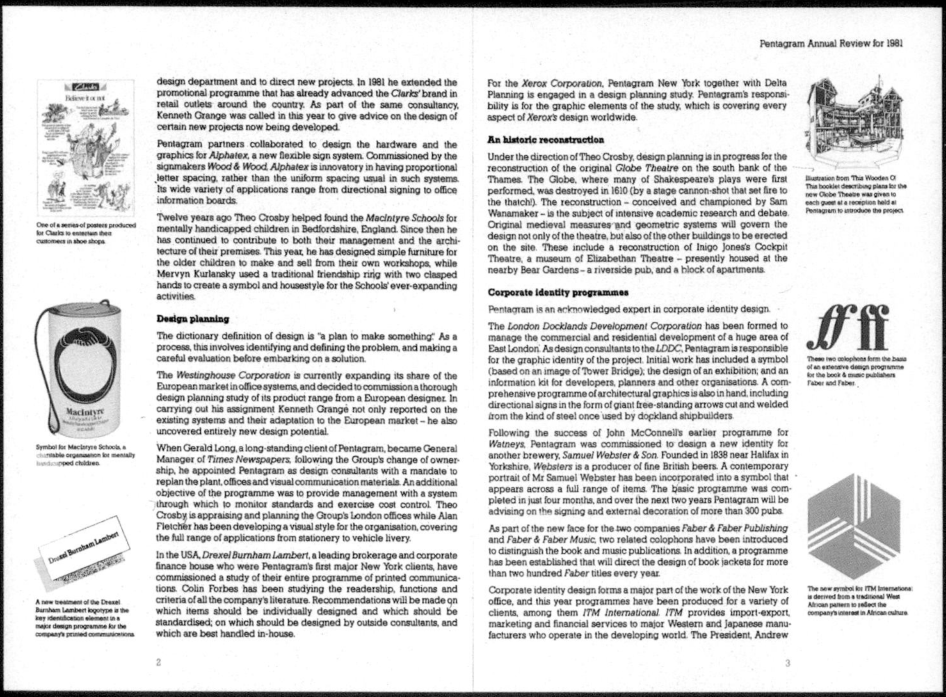

Pentagram Annual Review for 1981

design department and to direct new projects. In 1981 he extended the promotional programme that has already advanced the *Clarks'* brand in retail outlets around the country. As part of the same consultancy, Kenneth Grange was called in this year to give advice on the design of certain new projects now being developed.

Pentagram partners collaborated to design the hardware and the graphics for *Alphatex*, a new flexible sign system. Commissioned by the signmakers *Wood & Wood*, *Alphatex* is innovatory in having proportional letter spacing, rather than the uniform spacing usual in such systems. Its wide variety of applications range from directional signing to office information boards.

Twelve years ago Theo Crosby helped found the *MacIntyre Schools* for mentally handicapped children in Bedfordshire, England. Since then he has continued to contribute to both their management and the architecture of their premises. This year, he has designed simple furniture for the older children to make and sell from their own workshops, while Mervyn Kurlansky used a traditional friendship ring with two clasped hands to create a symbol and housestyle for the Schools' ever-expanding activities.

One of a series of posters produced for Clarks to entertain their customers in shoe shops.

Design planning

The dictionary definition of design is "a plan to make something." As a process, this involves identifying and defining the problem, and making a careful evaluation before embarking on a solution.

The *Westinghouse Corporation* is currently expanding its share of the European market in office systems, and decided to commission a thorough design planning study of its product range from a European designer. In carrying out his assignment Kenneth Grange not only reported on the existing systems and their adaptation to the European market – he also uncovered entirely new design potential.

Symbol for MacIntyre Schools, a charitable organisation for mentally handicapped children.

When Gerald Long, a long-standing client of Pentagram, became General Manager of *Times Newspapers*, following the Group's change of ownership, he appointed Pentagram as design consultants with a mandate to replan the plant, offices and visual communication materials. An additional objective of the programme was to provide management with a system through which to monitor standards and exercise cost control. Theo Crosby is appraising and planning the Group's London offices while Alan Fletcher has been developing a visual style for the organisation, covering the full range of applications from stationery to vehicle livery.

In the USA, *Drexel Burnham Lambert*, a leading brokerage and corporate finance house who were Pentagram's first major New York clients, have commissioned a study of their entire programme of printed communications. Colin Forbes has been studying the readership, functions and criteria of all the company's literature. Recommendations will be made on which items should be individually designed and which should be standardised; on which should be designed by outside consultants, and which are best handled in-house.

A new treatment of the Drexel Burnham Lambert logotype is the key identification element in a major design programme for the company's printed communications.

2

For the *Xerox Corporation*, Pentagram New York together with Delta Planning is engaged in a design planning study. Pentagram's responsibility is for the graphic elements of the study, which is covering every aspect of *Xerox's* design worldwide.

An historic reconstruction

Under the direction of Theo Crosby, design planning is in progress for the reconstruction of the original *Globe Theatre* on the south bank of the Thames. The Globe, where many of Shakespeare's plays were first performed, was destroyed in 1610 (by a stage cannon-shot that set fire to the thatch!). The reconstruction – conceived and championed by Sam Wanamaker – is the subject of intensive academic research and debate. Original medieval measures and geometric systems will govern the design not only of the theatre, but also of the other buildings to be erected on the site. These include a reconstruction of Inigo Jones's Cockpit Theatre, a museum of Elizabethan Theatre – presently housed at the nearby Bear Gardens – a riverside pub, and a block of apartments.

Illustration from This Wooden O! This booklet describing plans for the new Globe Theatre was given to each guest at a reception held at Pentagram to introduce the project.

Corporate identity programmes

Pentagram is an acknowledged expert in corporate identity design.

The *London Docklands Development Corporation* has been formed to manage the commercial and residential development of a huge area of East London. As design consultants to the *LDDC*, Pentagram is responsible for the graphic identity of the project. Initial work has included a symbol (based on an image of Tower Bridge); the design of an exhibition; and an information kit for developers, planners and other organisations. A comprehensive programme of architectural graphics is also in hand, including directional signs in the form of giant free-standing arrows cut and welded from the kind of steel once used by dockland shipbuilders.

These two colophons form the basis of an extensive design programme for the book & music publishers Faber and Faber.

Following the success of John McConnell's earlier programme for *Watneys*, Pentagram was commissioned to design a new identity for another brewery, *Samuel Webster & Son*. Founded in 1838 near Halifax in Yorkshire, *Websters* is a producer of fine British beers. A contemporary portrait of Mr Samuel Webster has been incorporated into a symbol that appears across a full range of items. The basic programme was completed in just four months, and over the next two years Pentagram will be advising on the signing and external decoration of more than 300 pubs.

As part of the new face for the two companies *Faber & Faber Publishing* and *Faber & Faber Music*, two related colophons have been introduced to distinguish the book and music publications. In addition, a programme has been established that will direct the design of book jackets for more than two hundred *Faber* titles every year.

Corporate identity design forms a major part of the work of the New York office, and this year programmes have been produced for a variety of clients, among them *ITM International*. *ITM* provides import-export, marketing and financial services to major Western and Japanese manufacturers who operate in the developing world. The President, Andrew

The new symbol for ITM International is derived from a traditional West African pattern to reflect the company's interest in African culture.

3

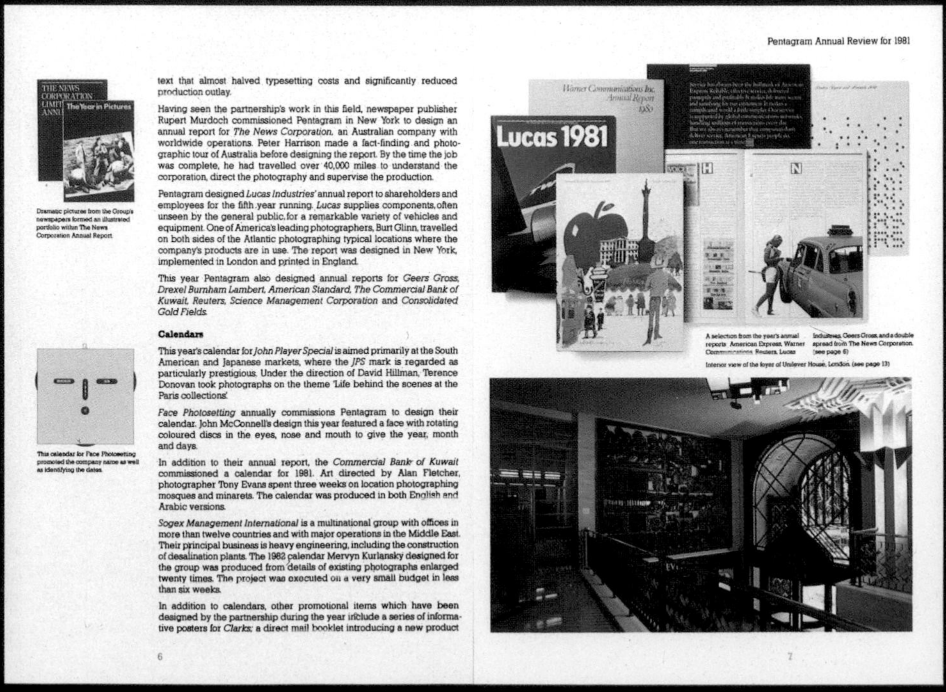

Pentagram Annual Review for 1981

text that almost halved typesetting costs and significantly reduced production outlay.

Having seen the partnership's work in this field, newspaper publisher Rupert Murdoch commissioned Pentagram in New York to design an annual report for *The News Corporation*, an Australian company with worldwide operations. Peter Harrison made a fact-finding and photographic tour of Australia before designing the report. By the time the job was complete, he had travelled over 40,000 miles to understand the corporation, direct the photography and supervise the production.

Dramatic pictures from the Group's newspapers formed an illustrated portfolio within The News Corporation Annual Report.

Pentagram designed *Lucas Industries'* annual report to shareholders and employees for the fifth year running. *Lucas* supplies components, often unseen by the general public, for a remarkable variety of vehicles and equipment. One of America's leading photographers, Burt Glinn, travelled on both sides of the Atlantic photographing typical locations where the company's products are in use. The report was designed in New York, implemented in London and printed in England.

This year Pentagram also designed annual reports for *Geers Gross*, *Drexel Burnham Lambert*, *American Standard*, *The Commercial Bank of Kuwait*, *Reuters*, *Science Management Corporation* and *Consolidated Gold Fields*.

Calendars

This year's calendar for *John Player Special* is aimed primarily at the South American and Japanese markets, where the *JPS* mark is regarded as particularly prestigious. Under the direction of David Hillman, Terence Donovan took photographs on the theme 'Life behind the scenes at the Paris collections'.

Face Photosetting annually commissions Pentagram to design their calendar. John McConnell's design this year featured a face with rotating coloured discs in the eyes, nose and mouth to give the year, month and days.

This calendar for Face Photosetting promoted the company name as well as identifying the dates.

In addition to their annual report, the *Commercial Bank of Kuwait* commissioned a calendar for 1981. Art directed by Alan Fletcher, photographer Tony Evans spent three weeks on location photographing mosques and minarets. The calendar was produced in both English and Arabic versions.

Sogex Management International is a multinational group with offices in more than twelve countries and with major operations in the Middle East. Their principal business is heavy engineering, including the construction of desalination plants. The 1982 calendar Mervyn Kurlansky designed for the group was produced from details of existing photographs enlarged twenty times. The project was executed on a very small budget in less than six weeks.

In addition to calendars, other promotional items which have been designed by the partnership during the year include a series of informative posters for *Clarks*; a direct mail booklet introducing a new product

6

A selection from the year's annual reports: American Express, Warner Communications, Reuters, Lucas Industries, Geers Gross, and a double spread from The News Corporation. (see page 6)

Interior view of the foyer of Unilever House, London. (see page 13)

7

Pirtle Design

Pirtle Design produces an annual look at its projects in the form of a calendar. Interspersed with text pages carrying the calendar are coated pages with portfolio pieces from the last year.
Audience: *Corporate and advertising*
Description: *7¼" x 11½", 48-page booklet*
Quantity: *1,500*

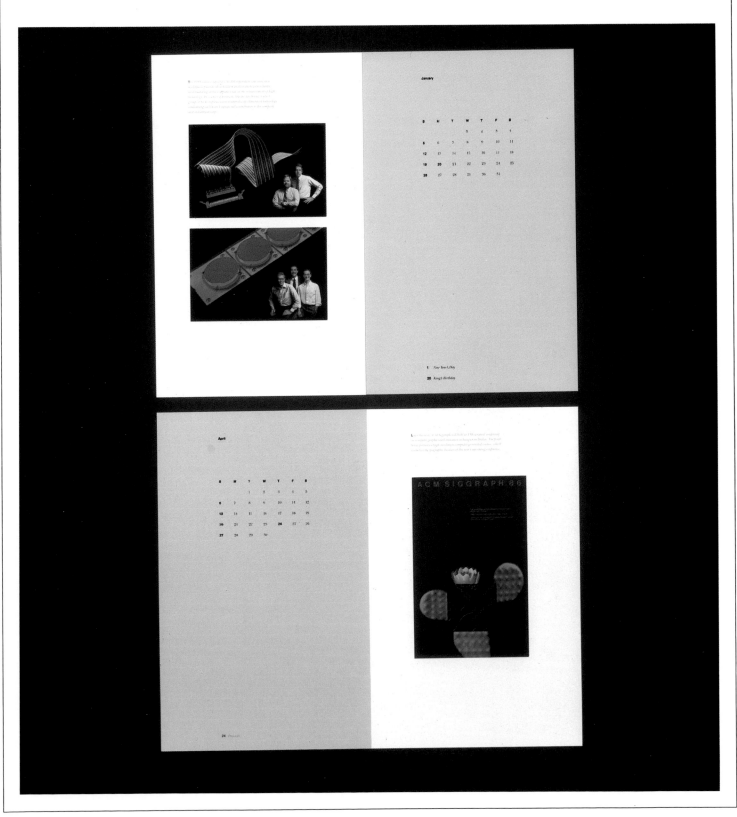

William Coupon Photography

The posters of William Coupon are interesting portfolio examples not only because of the images, but also because of the way in which they are reproduced. The rich color portraits of characters and celebrities as well as the large scale black & white portrait of David Byrne are printed by the rarely used colotype process. Colotype does not use dots, but rather layers of continuous color. This process enhances the collectable nature of William's posters.

Audience: *Art directors and designers*
Description: *25" x 30" posters*
Quantity: *3,000*

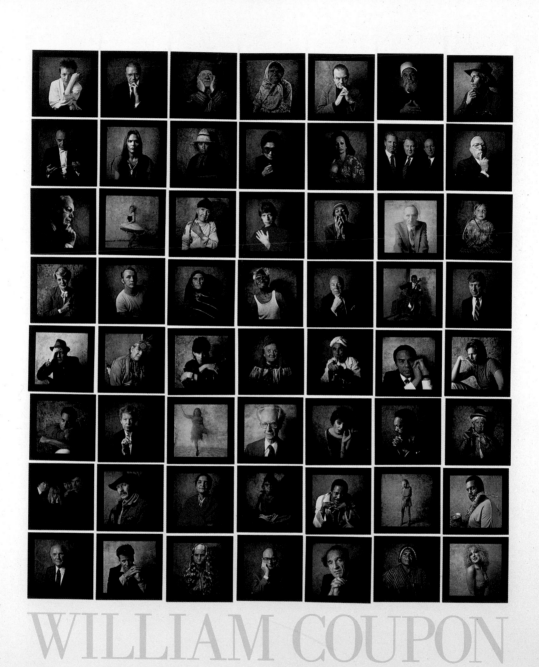

WILLIAM COUPON

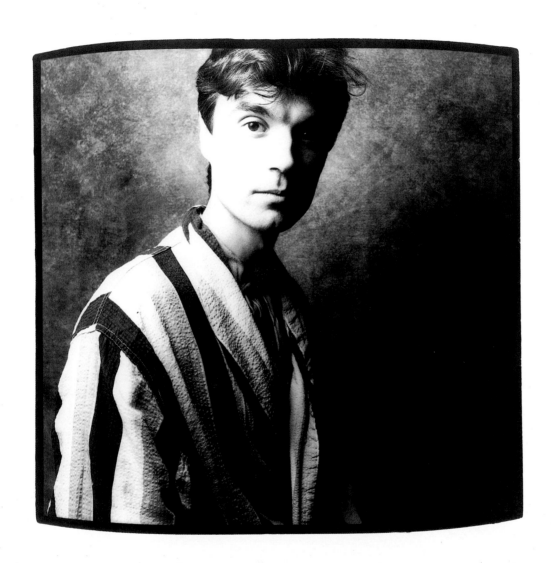

DAVID BYRNE

PHOTOGRAPHED BY WILLIAM COUPON

Bill Nelson

Virginia illustrator Bill Nelson has consistently promoted his image. His oversized (10" x 13") letterhead serves as a sampler of his "style," with objects and sketches surrounding the area for copy.

The posters that Bill uses to promote himself are based on work that he has drawn for himself. When organizations come to him for images, yet have very low budgets, Bill allows them to use existing images with the understanding that he will receive 1,000 to

1,500 overprints. The series of clown posters was developed in this manner.

Audience: *Art directors and designers*
Description: *10" x 13" four-color stationery*
Description: *Four-color posters in a range of sizes*
Quantity: *Varies*

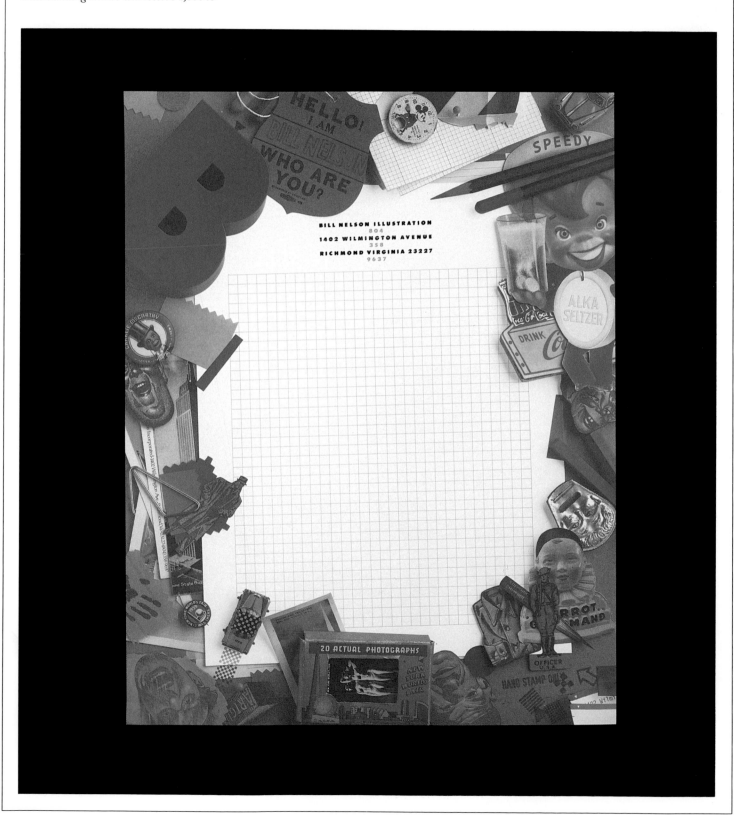

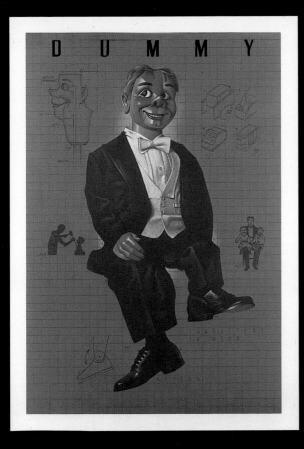

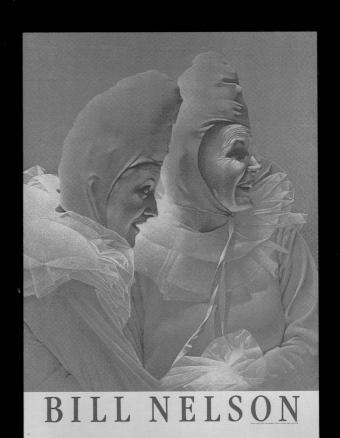

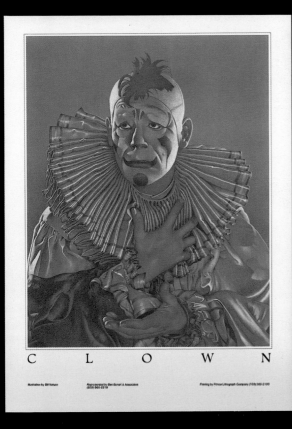

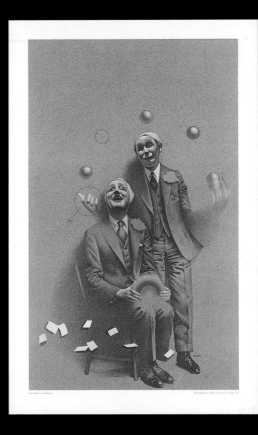

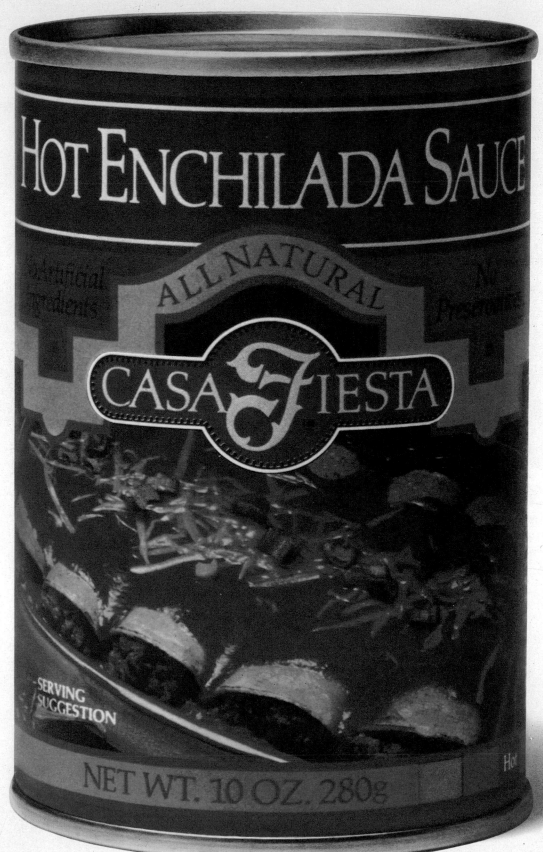

Sidjakov Berman & Gomez

To market the firm's packaging design, Sidjakov Berman & Gomez designed three large (16½" x 22") newsprint mailers. The sheets were folded down to fit in a 8½" x 11" envelope and mailed to 3,000 existing clients and new business prospects. The mailings focused on the food and packaging trade, as well as prospects for corporate identities. The three mailers were sent at one-month intervals. The appeal of the mailers was the use of scale—with the package dominating the mailer—played off against interesting headlines: "We designed the whole enchilada."

Audience: *Corporate and food industry*
Description: *16½" x 22" newsprint mailers*
Quantity: *5,000*

Tom Curry, Illustrator

When Tom Curry's rep suggested the idea of a 3-D viewer, he didn't see why not. The illustrator's work was put on the viewer discs and used as a leave-behind by both Tom and the rep. "When my rep called on people, he left them a viewer as well," says Tom. "I just sent out the disc. It certainly got a lot of reaction."

Audience: *Art directors and designers*
Description: *3-D disc*
Quantity: *2,000*

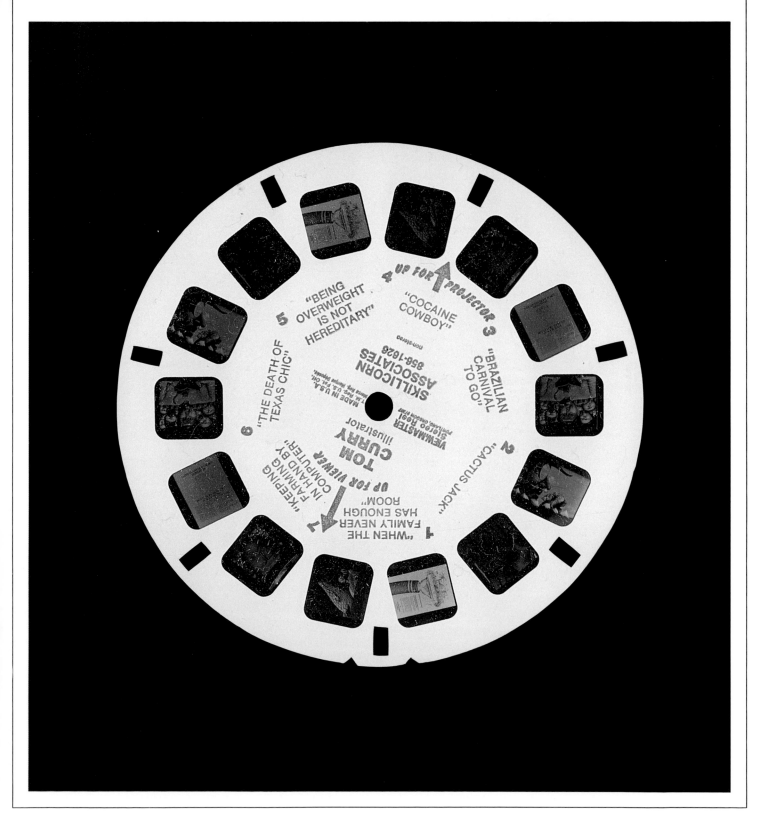

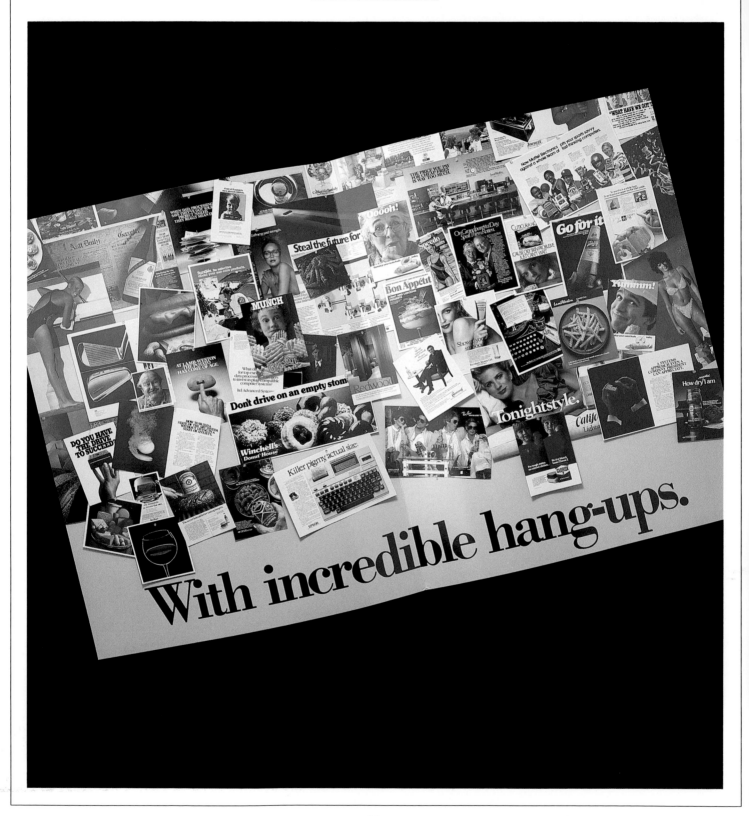

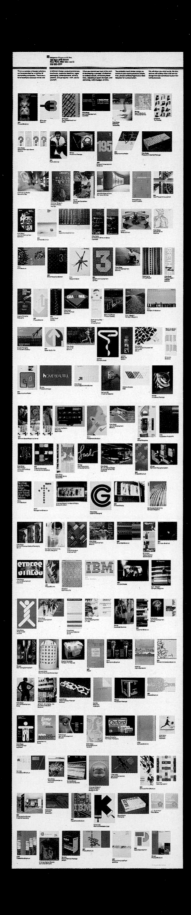

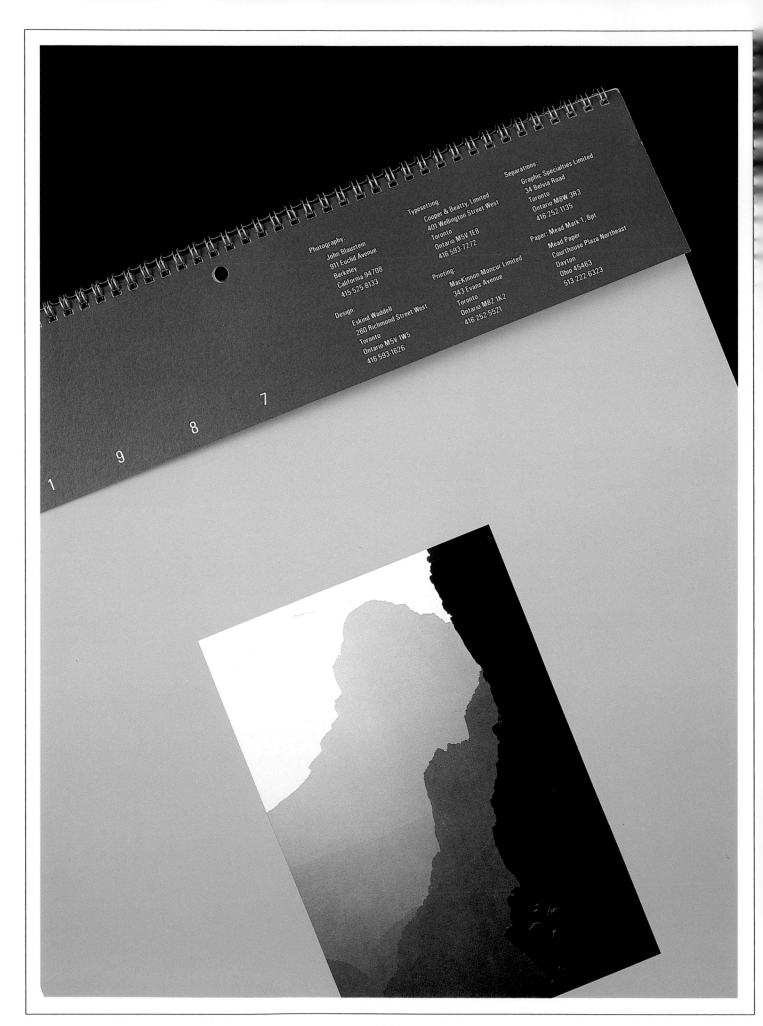

Photography:
John Blaustein
911 Euclid Avenue
Berkeley
California 94708
415 525-8133

Design:
Eskind Waddell
260 Richmond Street West
Toronto
Ontario M5V 1W5
416 593-1626

Typesetting:
Cooper & Beatty, Limited
401 Wellington Street West
Toronto
Ontario M5V 1E8
416 593-7272

Printing:
MacKinnon-Moncur Limited
343 Evans Avenue
Toronto
Ontario M8Z 1K2
416 252-5521

Separations:
Graphic Specialties Limited
34 Belvia Road
Toronto
Ontario M8W 3R3
416 252-1135

Paper: Mead Mark 1, 8pt
Mead Paper
Courthouse Plaza Northeast
Dayton
Ohio 45463
513 222-6323

CREATIVE PARTNERSHIPS

Let's say you are a designer. You've got a great idea for a self-promotion. Who's going to write it? Are you as good a writer as you are a designer? Do you want writing work? Probably not. How about photography or illustration? Same question. Same answer? Why not organize a creative team and produce a promotion that benefits all of you? Or you could swap your design efforts for their writing, photography, or illustration. Of course, if you are thinking about a print campaign, you're going to need typesetting and printing. Why not put these people on your team, too—or work out a swap. Most people will be receptive if you convince them that there is something in it for them.

A very good example of a creative promotion—put together by a team—that has benefited all the parties involved is an annual calendar project produced by Canadian designers Roslyn Eskind and Malcolm Waddell. The calendar is a showpiece for the design firm, Eskind Waddell, and the photographer, Californian John Blaustein. That you could assume. But the calendar is also a hardworking promotion for the typesetter, printer, color separator, and paper merchant, all of whom are prominently credited.

There are many opportunities for creative partnerships, if you just keep your mind and ears open to opportunity. For designers, a fertile area to find photographers who may be in the market for a creative trade out is the portfolio review. Every week photographers call on design studios to show their work. Many are in real need of promotional materials but do not have any contacts with typesetters or printers, or may not feel confident enough to ask a designer to work with them. At the same time, most design studios are in constant need of photography to promote themselves.

The same can be said for the illustrator/designer and writer/designer relationships, although the photographer/designer partnership seems to be the most prevalent.

There are also unique partnerships that should not be overlooked. Raphaele, a chrome retoucher, was the central figure in a partnership that included a design firm, a photographer, and a printer (page 95). All three firms regularly use the retouching services of Raphaele, thus making the trade out inviting. The added incentive for working on Raphaele's project was the chance to have a part in producing an award winning poster. For many creative partnerships, the opportunity to produce award winning work makes the business considerations all the more workable.

Eskind Waddell
John Blaustein
The 1987 joint venture calendar featured John Blaustein's personal photographs of the Grand Canyon.
Audience: *Corporate and design firms*
Description: *17" x 23", 14-sheet calendar*
Quantity: *3,000*

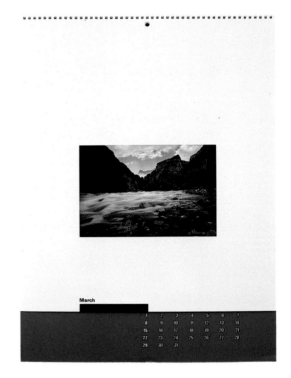

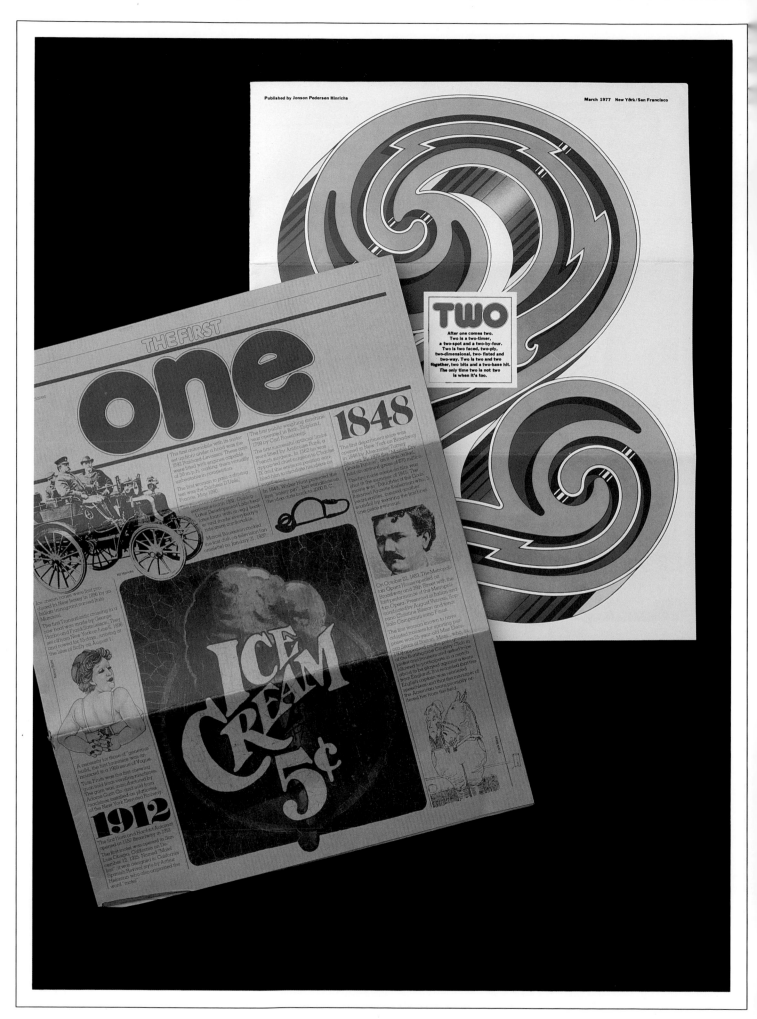

Jonson Pedersen Hinrichs

In 1977 Jonson Pedersen Hinrichs produced tabloids to promote the firm, while giving ample credit to the artists that contributed to the projects. The back page of the tabloid (shown below), listed the names and telephone numbers of the contributors.

The firm (now the West Coast office of Pentagram) doesn't produce this form of self-promotion any longer, and for good reason. "We now find ourselves getting to do these type of projects for hire and don't feel the need to do our own."

Audience: *Corporate*
Description: *11" x 14" two-color, 8-page tabloids*
Quantity: *1,500*

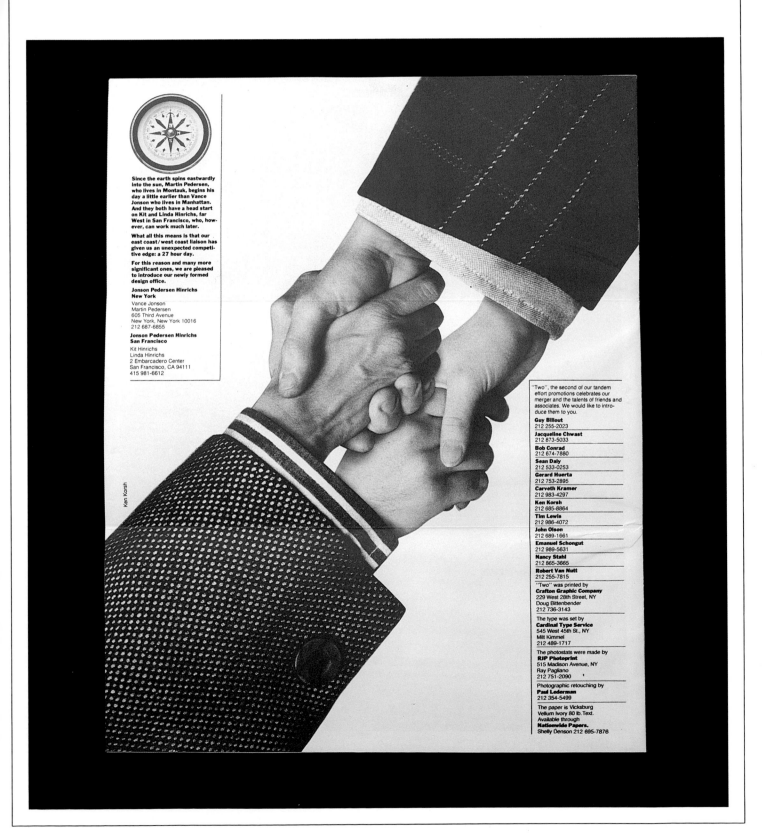

Since the earth spins eastwardly into the sun, Martin Pedersen, who lives in Montauk, begins his day a little earlier than Vance Jonson who lives in Manhattan. And they both have a head start on Kit and Linda Hinrichs, far West in San Francisco, who, however, can work much later.

What all this means is that our east coast/west coast liaison has given us an unexpected competitive edge: a 27 hour day.

For this reason and many more significant ones, we are pleased to introduce our newly formed design office.

Jonson Pedersen Hinrichs
New York

Vance Jonson
Martin Pedersen
605 Third Avenue
New York, New York 10016
212 687-6855

Jonson Pedersen Hinrichs
San Francisco

Kit Hinrichs
Linda Hinrichs
2 Embarcadero Center
San Francisco, CA 94111
415 981-6612

Ken Korsh

"Two", the second of our tandem effort promotions celebrates our merger and the talents of friends and associates. We would like to introduce them to you.

Guy Billout
212 255-2023
Jacqueline Chwast
212 873-5033
Bob Conrad
212 674-7880
Sean Daly
212 533-0253
Gerard Huerta
212 753-2895
Carveth Kramer
212 983-4297
Ken Korsh
212 685-8864
Tim Lewis
212 986-4072
John Olson
212 689-1661
Emanuel Schongut
212 989-5631
Nancy Stahl
212 865-3665
Robert Van Nutt
212 255-7815

"Two" was printed by
Crafton Graphic Company
229 West 28th Street, NY
Doug Bittenbender
212 736-3143

The type was set by
Cardinal Type Service
545 West 45th St., NY
Milt Kimmel
212 489-1717

The photostats were made by
RJP Photoprint
515 Madison Avenue, NY
Ray Pagliano
212 751-2090

Photographic retouching by
Paul Lederman
212 354-5499

The paper is Vicksburg
Vellum Ivory 80 lb. Text.
Available through
Nationwide Papers.
Shelly Denson 212 695-7876

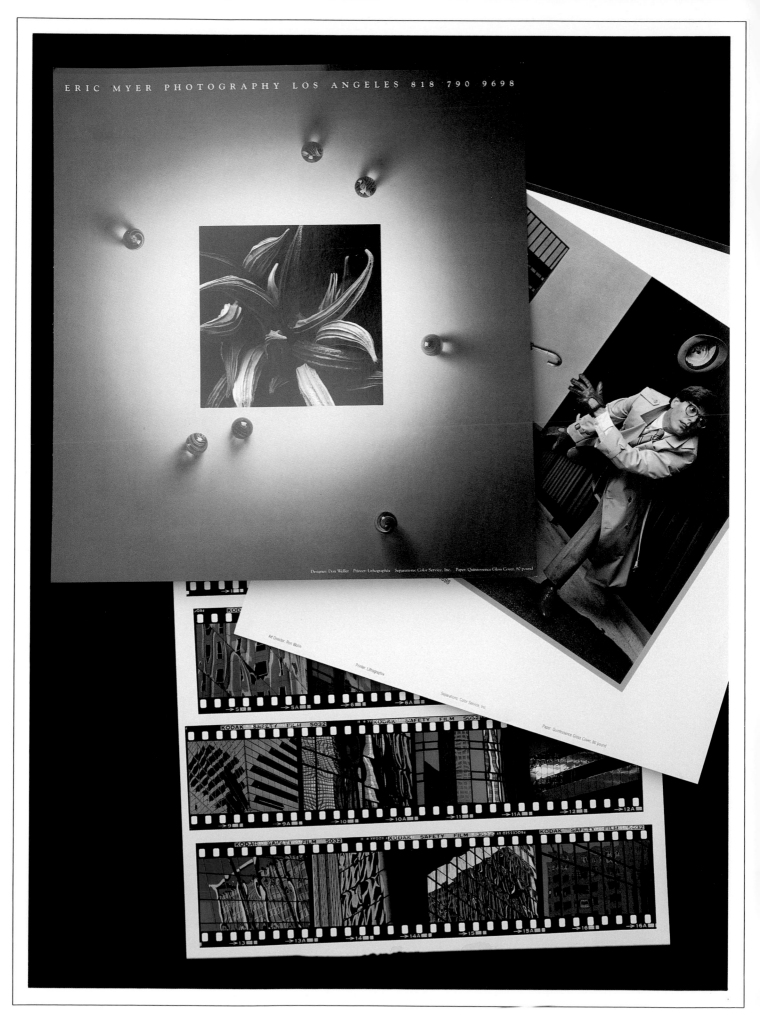

ERIC MYER PHOTOGRAPHY LOS ANGELES 818 790 9698

Designer: Don Weller Printer: Lithographix Separations: Color Service, Inc. Paper: Quintessence Gloss Cover, 80 pound

Art Director: Ron Wolin

Printer: Lithographix

Separations: Color Service, Inc.

Paper: Quintessence Gloss Cover, 80 pound

Eric Myer Photography

Los Angeles photographer Eric Myer approaches his self-promotion mailers much the same way he works on projects: with an art director or designer. Eric asks creatives that he works with to be "guest designers" for his promotional mailers. They conceive and lay out the page keeping to a standard size, and then work with Eric to illustrate it with photographs. Each mailer has the look of the individual designer, displaying Eric's photographic solutions.

Audience: *Art directors and designers*
Description: *11" x 12" full-color sheets*
Quantity: *2,000*

Raphaele Chrome Retouching

The Raphaele Chrome Retouching Contest challenged art directors and designers to find the ten or eleven areas in a photograph that had been altered by Raphaele. The poster, which was done on a trade-out basis with the photographer, designer and printer, featured an image made up of three photographs (the entire scene, the male model and the smoke). Recipients of the poster were asked to list the "retouched" areas—such as the wax being duplicated on the candelabras or the grapes on the plate being repeated in different sizes—

with the winner awarded a case of wine at a later party.
Audience: *Art directors and designers*
Description: *20" x 26" full-color poster with gold stamping*
Quantity: *2,000*

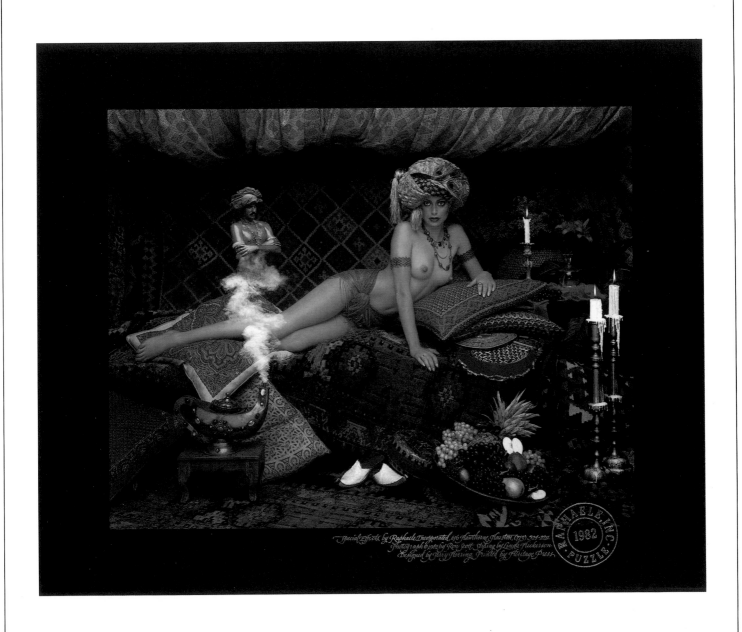

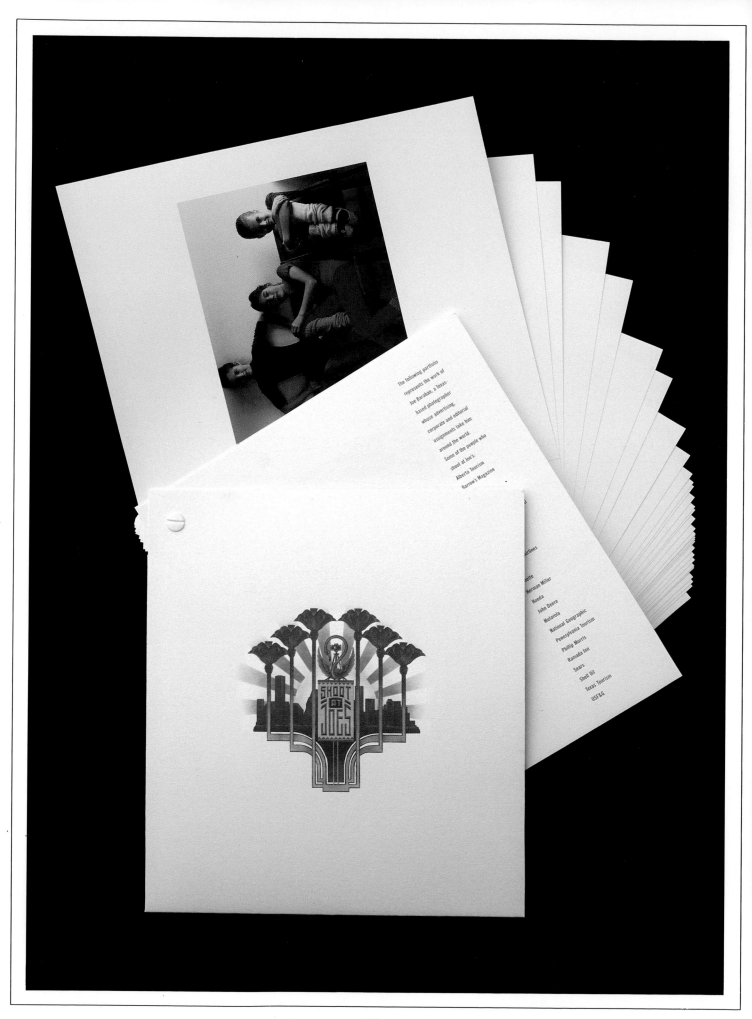

Joe Baraban Photography

The self-promotion portfolio for Joe Baraban Photography was a three-way trade between the photographer, design firm, and printer. Each firm provided service to one another on individual projects for the design firm and printer, in addition to Joe's piece.

The portfolio Joe sends out is a boxed, post bound set of 32 individual photographs printed on slick, coated paper. A cover sheet carrying a brief statement and partial list of clients is printed on uncoated, text paper. The last page, also on text paper, lists the studio's address, the address of the rep, and credits for the design firm, cover illustrator, printer, color separator and paper.

Audience: Corporate, advertising agencies and design firms
Description: Thirty-four 8½" x 9½" sheets, post bound, boxed
Quantity: 2,000

Jim Jacobs' Studio
Pirtle Design

This Christmas card for two Dallas design firms started as a concept by Woody Pirtle. He showed the concept to Jim Jacobs and it was Jim's idea that made the card work mechanically. From there, the project was a partnership. Each firm sent out cards to their clients and friends with their own firm name on it.

Audience: Friends and clients
Description: 4" x 9" card with pull-out
Quantity: 500

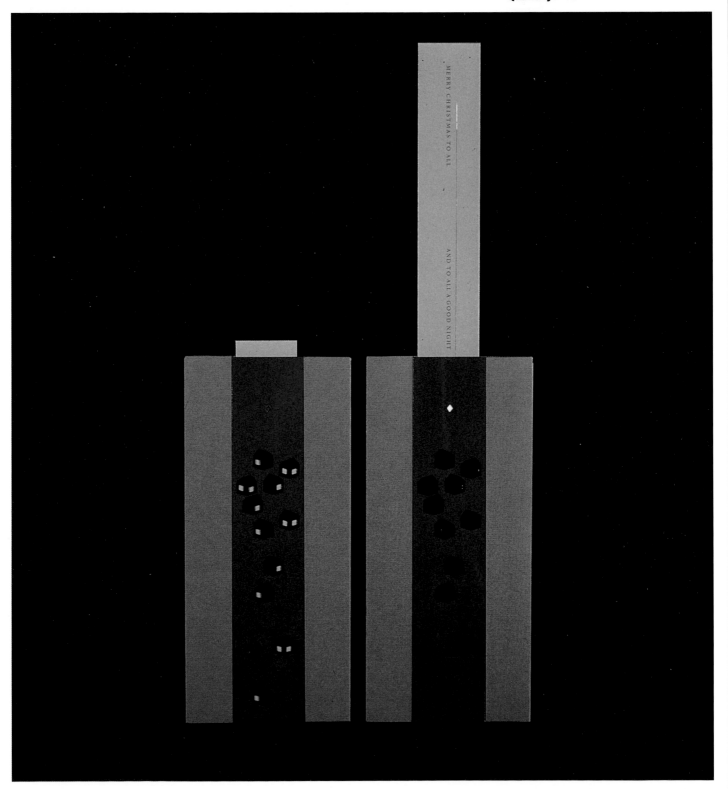

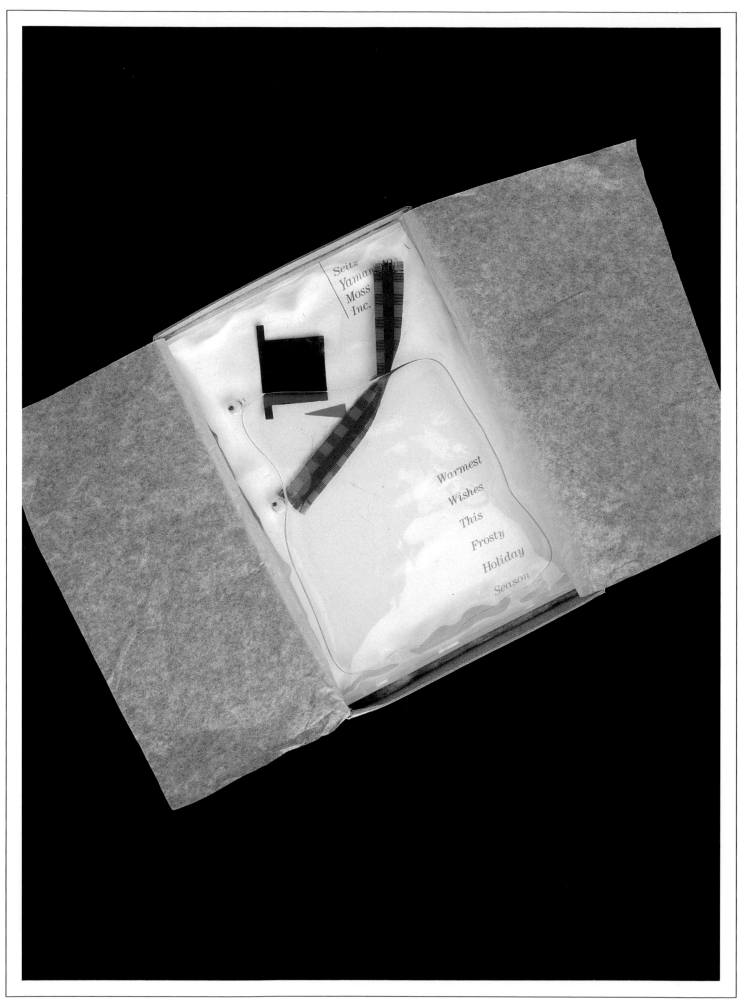

DO SOMETHING SPECIAL

Seitz Yamamoto Moss
Audience: *Clients and friends*
Description: *4" x 6" box with water-filled acrylic bag*
Quantity: *500*

While the portfolio piece is the backbone of any self-promotion campaign, the "special" piece is the one that gets people talking. These are the pieces that you do when you "just want to do something." It may be an excuse to show how creative you are, or it may respond to a real need. But whatever the reason, when creative people decide to do something "special," it usually is.

Since this category of promotion is by its very nature soft-sell, it is usually practiced by people who are trying to enhance an image, rather than make one. While these efforts can lead to work, asking for business is not the primary concern. One of the benefits of this type of promotional piece is that when you do something that is meant to please, it is usually a very real reflection on the persons esthetic judgment. And that can lead to work.

The need to keep in touch with clients, potential clients, contacts and friends is reason enough to "do something." One of better success stories on how to "keep in touch" is the *Pentagram Papers* (page 100), the ongoing self-publishing effort by the London/New York/San Francisco design firm, Pentagram. The booklets that comprise the series all deal with different subject matter, presented in the same format. The series began in 1975 and continues today. The *Pentagram Papers* are a model for creative self-promotion, the ingredients of which can serve as a basic guideline for any concerted promotion campaign:

Have an idea, a concept.
Execute the concept in a fresh way.
Be interesting. Not just to people in the business, but to a broader audience as well.
Involve other creative disciplines.
Produce the promotions with some regularity.
Create memorability. Make the promotion too valuable to throw away.

While the *Pentagram Papers* are part of a series and utilize a continuing format, these need not be major considerations. The one-time effort of Seitz Yamamoto Moss (opposite page) celebrating an unusually warm winter in Minneapolis is also a prototype of a successful promotion. With the exception of *regularity,* the guidelines detailed above could easily be applied to this unique mailer.

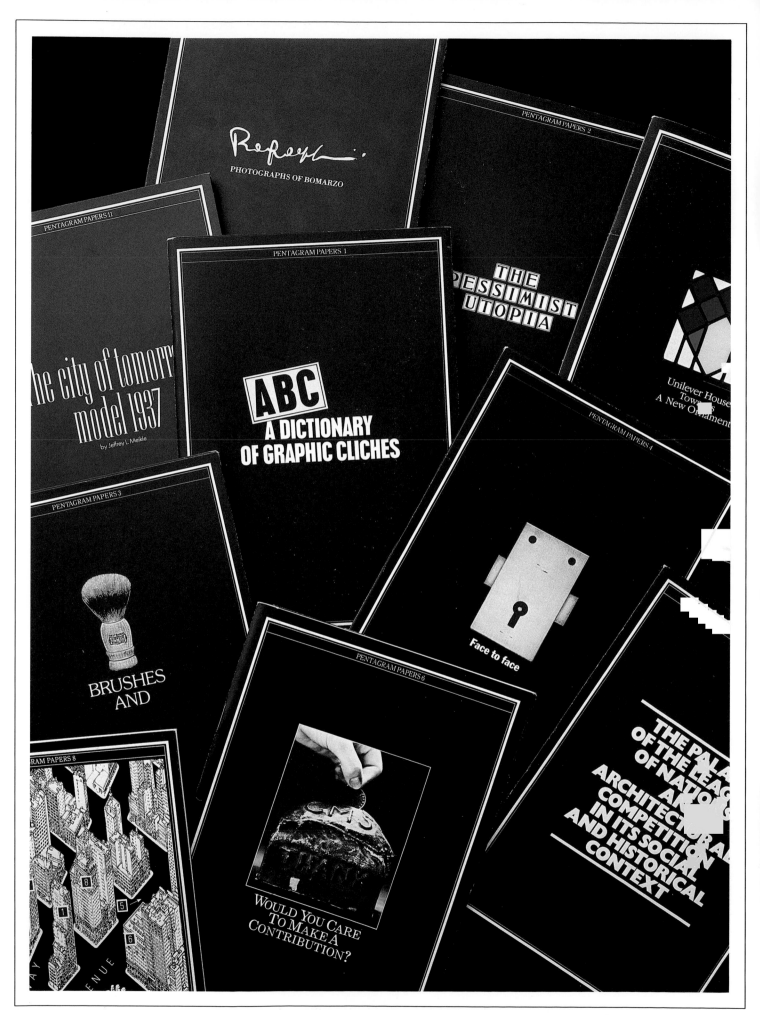

Pentagram Design

The statement that accompanies every issue of the Pentagram Papers *sums up the point of view of these unique booklets. "Pentagram Papers will publish, at regular intervals, examples of curious, entertaining, stimulating, provocative and occasionally controversial points of view that have come to the attention of, or in some cases are actually originated by, Pentagram."*

The idea for the Pentagram Papers originated from a 1975 conversation between *Pentagram Design partners Colin Forbes and John McConnell, as they sat on a train in Holland pondering the direction of their design firm. "We knew that we wanted to do something special. Wouldn't it be nice to show work that we valued, even work that we ourselves hadn't done," reflects Colin. "From there, John designed the format and became the editor."*

The Pentagram Papers *has become special, to the point that even the mailing list is not taken lightly. "We don't automatically send it to clients," says Colin, "and we (the firm) personally know everyone on the list."*

The subject matter for the Papers *has ranged from a photographic essay of objects that make faces (top) by Jean Edouard Robert to an essay on the refurbishment of Unilever House, London (bottom) by Theo Crosby.*
Audience: *Friends and clients*
Description: *5³⁄₄″ x 8¹⁄₄″ booklets*
Quantity: *1,500*

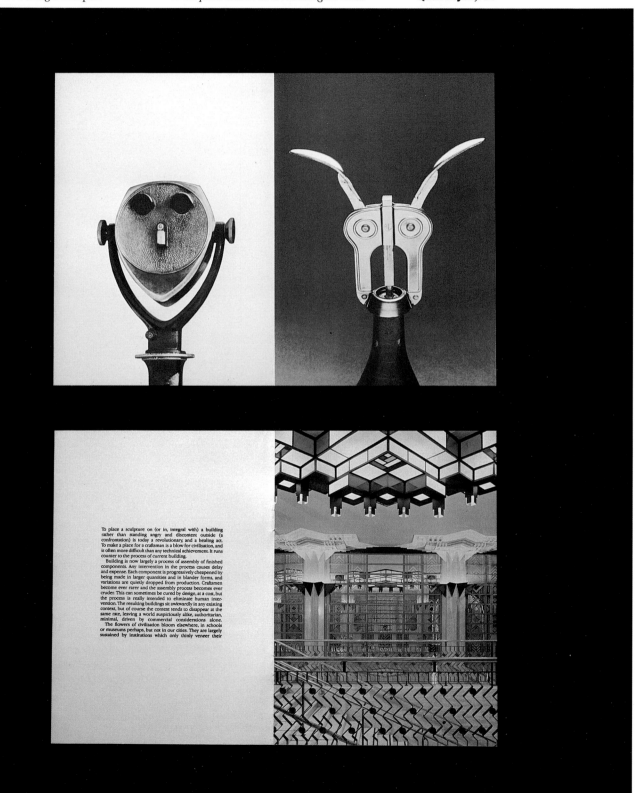

To place a sculpture on (or in, integral with) a building rather than standing angry and discontent outside (a confrontation) is today a revolutionary, and a healing act. To make a place for a craftsman is a blow for civilisation, and is often more difficult than any technical achievement. It runs counter to the process of current building.

Building is now largely a process of assembly of finished components. Any intervention in the process causes delay and expense. Each component is progressively cheapened by being made in larger quantities and in blander forms, and variations are quietly dropped from production. Craftsmen become ever rarer and the assembly process becomes ever cruder. This can sometimes be cured by design, at a cost, but the process is really intended to eliminate human intervention. The resulting buildings sit awkwardly in any existing context, but of course the context tends to disappear at the same rate, leaving a world suspiciously alike, authoritarian, minimal, driven by commercial considerations alone.

The flowers of civilisation bloom elsewhere, in schools or museums perhaps, but not in our cities. They are largely sustained by institutions which only thinly veneer their

Jeanmard Design & Illustration

"I always liked pennants," says illustrator Jerry Jeanmard. *"So when I saw that I could get 100 of these for under $100, I decided to do it. And I liked the color and the feel of the felt, and they were something that designers seemed to keep on their walls."* The Latin expression in the logo reads, *"My art for your money."*

Audience: *Art directors and designers*
Description: *24″ felt pennants*
Quantity: *100*

Sons of the Golden West Studio

Illustrator Robert Rodriguez gives this account of this unique promotion: "We had this rep come by from a Mexican calendar company, and we thought, 'Hey, that would be kind of neat.' We bought calendars from them for about three years. We could only give these to certain types of clients; after all, it wasn't even our illustration on the calendar. But it was a lot of fun. And they were cheap, around $1 apiece for a hundred calendars."

Audience: *Art directors and designers*
Description: *16″ x 35″ over-printed calendar*
Quantity: *100*

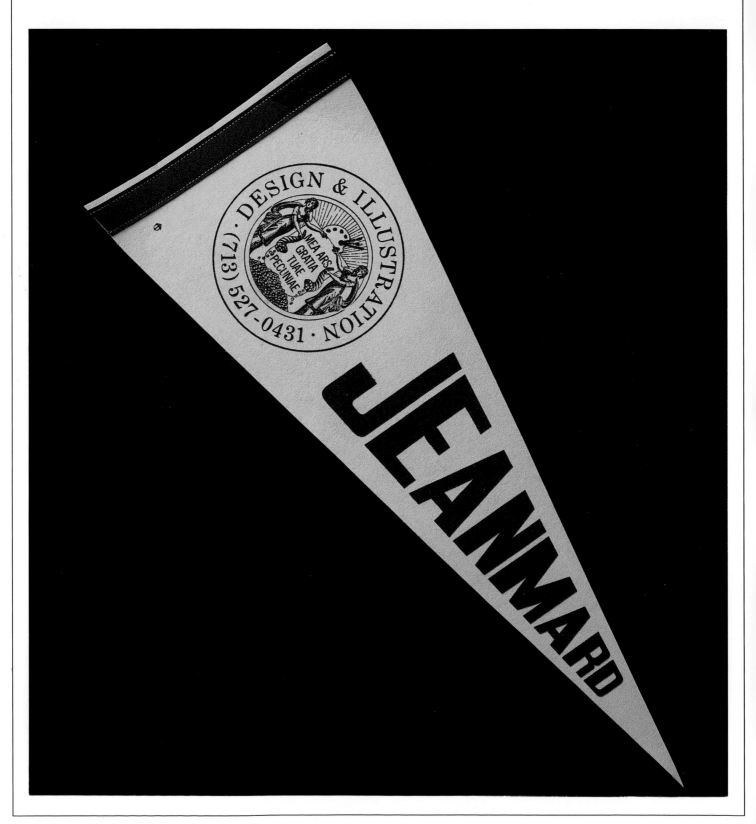

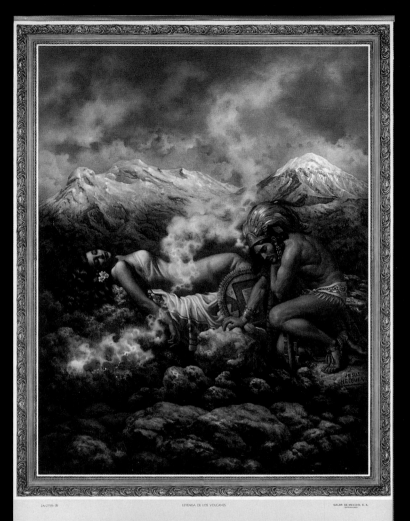

Reuben Njaa Photography

After photographing a project for art director Barbara Shimkus, San Antonio photographer Reuben Njaa offered to take Barbara's picture. Working with a makeup artist, Reuben produced a photograph that led to a photographic series of local designers and art directors. The people being photographed were clients, or soon became clients. For Reuben, who was new in town, the brochure designed by Barbara Shimkus became an instant entree into the local market.

Audience: *Art directors and designers*
Description: *9" x 12" full-color, 20-page brochure*
Quantity: *2,000*

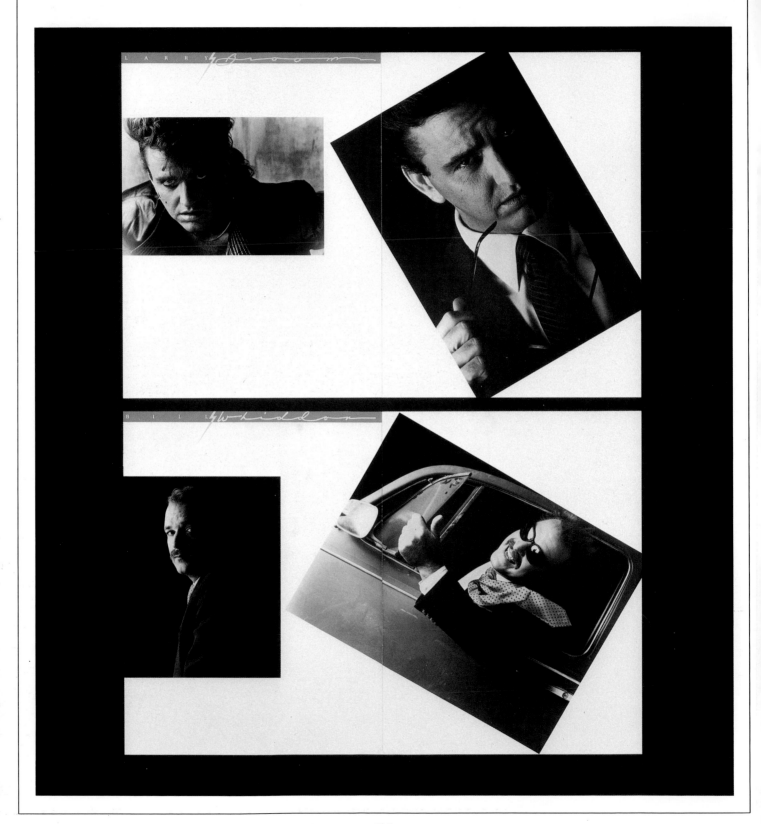

The Graphics Studio
Los Angeles designer Gerry Rosentswieg put together a team that could design, produce, illustrate, set type, make color separations, print, and bind a calendar that they could all use for their own promotion. The piece was a symphony of colorful illustrations with cut-outs, flaps and fold-outs. "We wanted to do a piece that was really a show piece for everyone," says Rosentswieg. "I would say that we did."

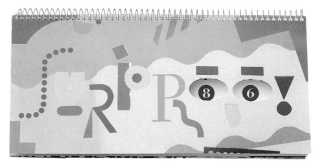

Audience: *Corporate, advertising agencies, paper companies, and design firms*
Description: *Sixty-seven 10½" x 5" spiral-bound sheets*
Quantity: *2,000*

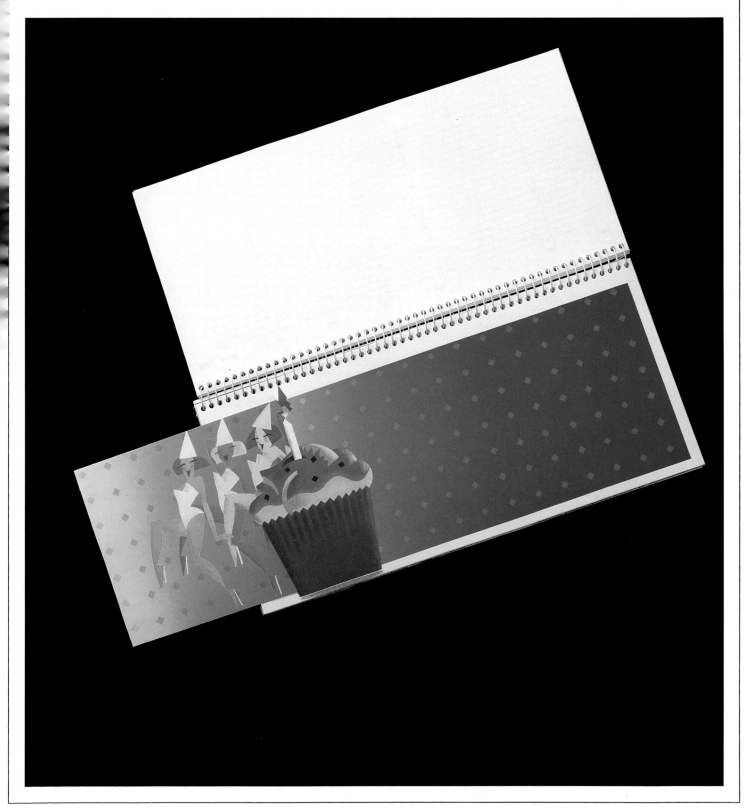

Steve Brady Photography

A poster for Steve Brady Photography listed the credits for projects Steve had produced over the past year. By listing the credits in a form reminiscent of awards shows, Steve was able to emphasize his clients in a form designers are very familiar with.
Audience: Art directors and designers
Description: 23" x 35" two-color poster
Quantity: 2,000

Nikolay Zurek Photography

With the help of designer Jerry Berman, Nikolay Zurek set out to produce a series of ads for one very special place, the back cover of Graphis magazine, published in Zurich, Switzerland. Playing off his name and his large portfolio of travel photography, Zurek published a series of ten ads that used a location photograph with his name as the fictional address. With a photograph from Germany, for instance, the headline is "Zurek, Germany."

"The ads were aimed at a broad audience," says Zurek, "and this was a unique way to associate my name with location photography."
Audience: Art directors and designers
Description: 9¼" x 11½" four-color ads
Quantity: Ten individual ads

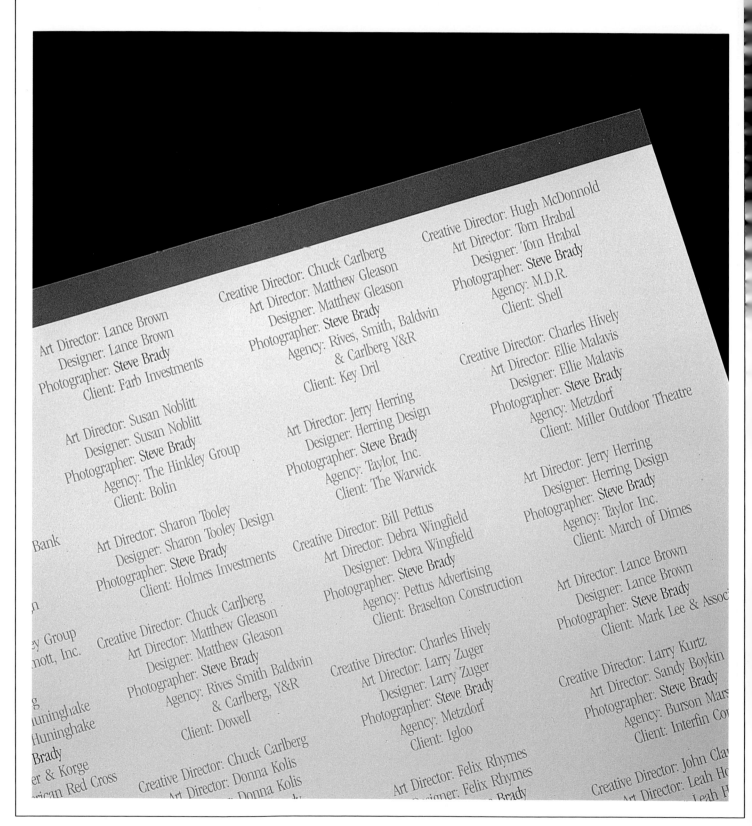

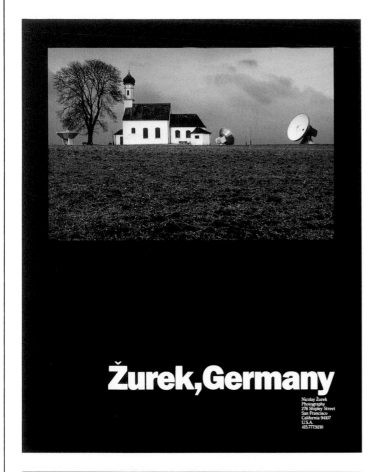

Žurek, Germany

Nicolay Žurek
Photography
276 Shipley Street
San Francisco
California 94107
U.S.A.
415.777.9210

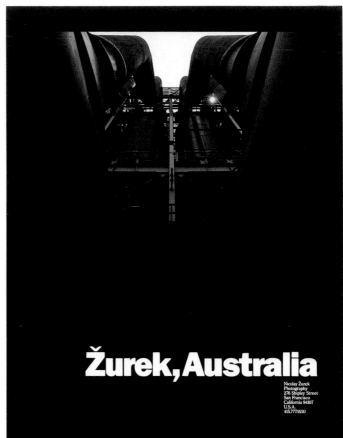

Žurek, Australia

Nicolay Žurek
Photography
276 Shipley Street
San Francisco
California 94107
U.S.A.
415.777.9210

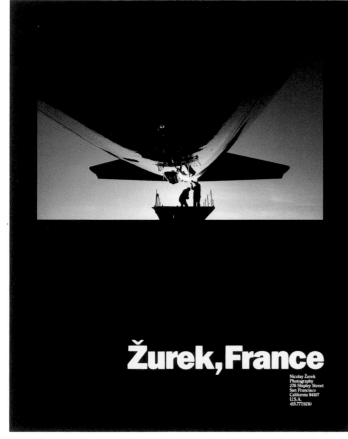

Žurek, France

Nicolay Žurek
Photography
276 Shipley Street
San Francisco
California 94107
U.S.A.
415.777.9210

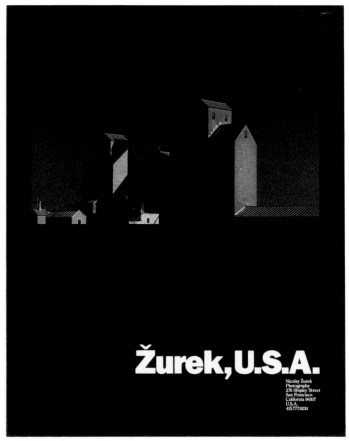

Žurek, U.S.A.

Nicolay Žurek
Photography
276 Shipley Street
San Francisco
California 94107
U.S.A.
415.777.9210

Pirtle Design

Sometimes you don't need much of a reason for self-publishing. From the opening copy for a booklet entitled "K-9" by Woody Pirtle:

"Dogs. Everybody loves them. From the poorest to the purest breeds, they hunt our game, lick our wounds, share our solitude and steal our hearts.

"On the following pages I am pleased to share with you a selection of nine private works as a tribute to man's best friend."

Audience: *Clients and friends*

Description: *6½" x 9½" four-color, 24-page booklet*

Quantity: *1,500*

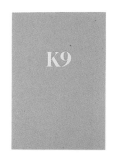

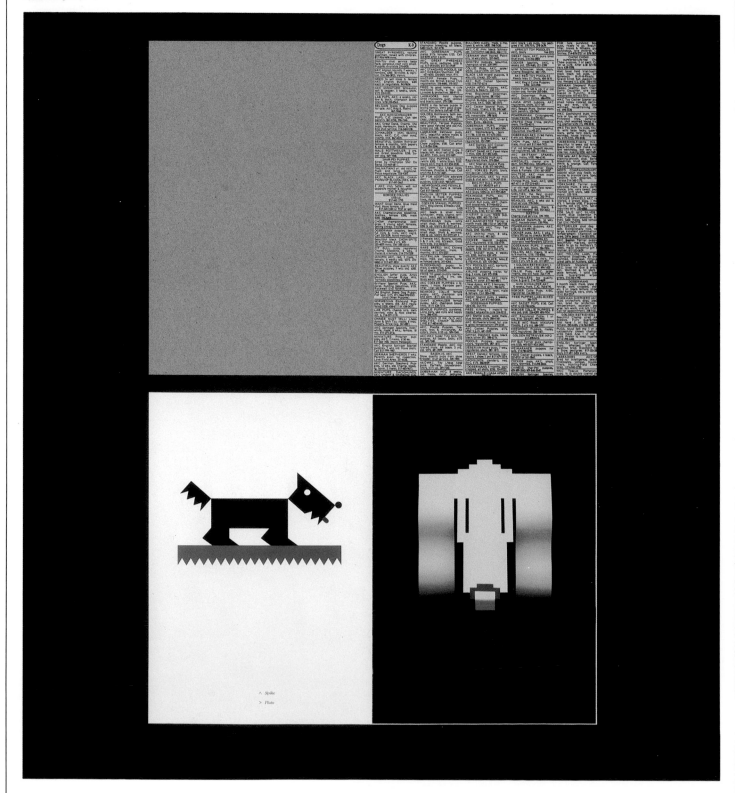

Cross Associates

After a year of traveling around the country and abroad, designer Jim Cross wanted to share with his friends the images of the people and places he had seen. Jim takes and prints his own photographs, so this booklet has a very personal touch. Small duo-tone photographs appear on coated paper across from very short captions on text paper.

Audience: *Clients, friends, and acquaintances*

Description: *5½" x 7" two-color, 64-page booklet*

Quantity: *500*

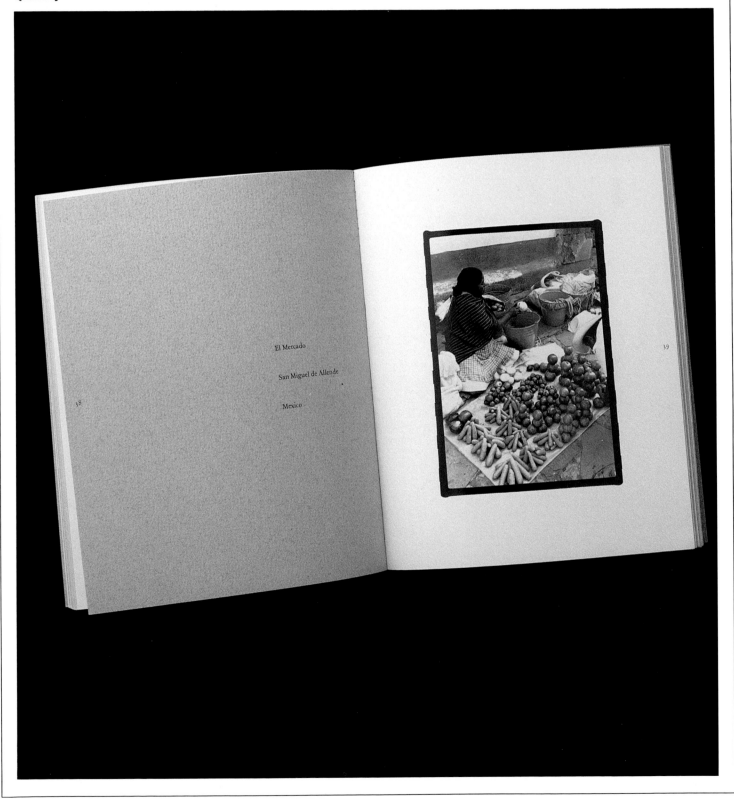

Robert Vogele, Inc.

Robert Vogele, Inc.'s brochure, designed by Jim Lienhart, was a thought-provoking look at the power, philosophy, and circumstances of trademarks. Titled "Heil Who?," the booklet probes the meanings and associations of images, while making a strong pitch for the value of good corporate identity.

Audience: *Corporate*
Description: *9" x 9" two-color, 20-page brochure*
Quantity: *5,000*

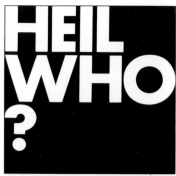

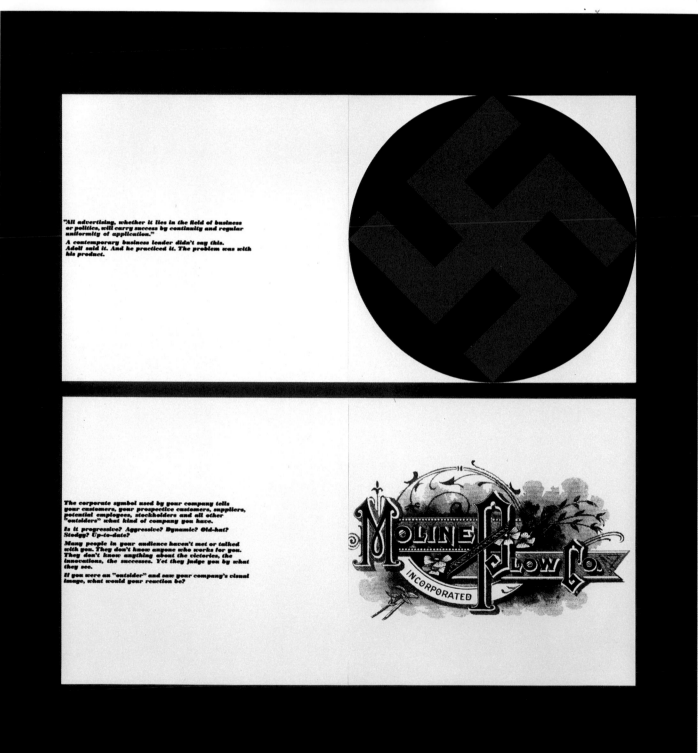

"All advertising, whether it lies in the field of business or politics, will carry success by continuity and regular uniformity of application."

A contemporary business leader didn't say this. Adolf said it. And he practiced it. The problem was with his product.

The corporate symbol used by your company tells your customers, your prospective customers, suppliers, potential employees, stockholders and all other "outsiders" what kind of company you have.

Is it progressive? Aggressive? Dynamic? Old-hat? Stodgy? Up-to-date?

Many people in your audience haven't met or talked with you. They don't know anyone who works for you. They don't know anything about the victories, the innovations, the successes. Yet they judge you by what they see.

If you were an "outsider" and saw your company's visual image, what would your reaction be?

Joe Baraban Photography

"Portraits" is a brochure of Joe Baraban's photography that was primarily produced as a sample of the work of a color separator. For consideration of his allowing the photographs to be used, Joe was provided with enough copies of the brochure for his mailing list.

Other than an opening and closing statement, only captions appear in the booklet. The portraits are printed on black backgrounds with a caption printed in a color that matches a color in the photograph.

Audience: *Art directors and designers*
Description: *7" x 10" four-color, 24-page brochure*
Quantity: *2,000*

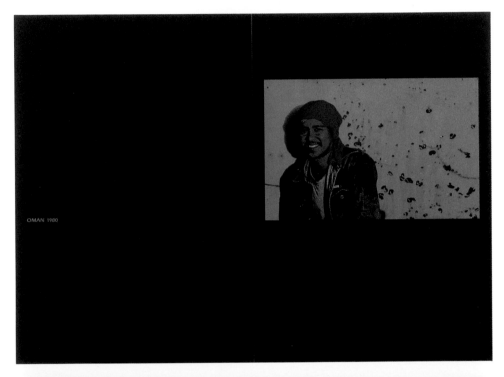

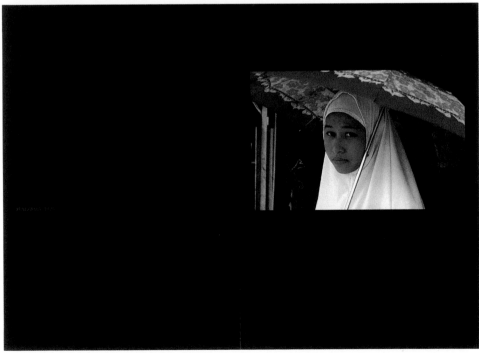

Gary McCoy

For years, Dallas photographer Gary McCoy has been taking infrared, black & white photographs of cacti as a personal project. So when he approached Dallas design firm Pirtle Design to produce a marketing piece, the personal project became a business promotion. The award winning brochure is used mainly as a one-on-one leave-behind.

Audience: *Art directors and designers*
Description: *12" x 12" black & white, 24-page brochure*
Quantity: *1,400*

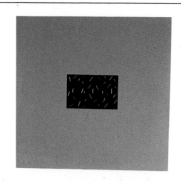

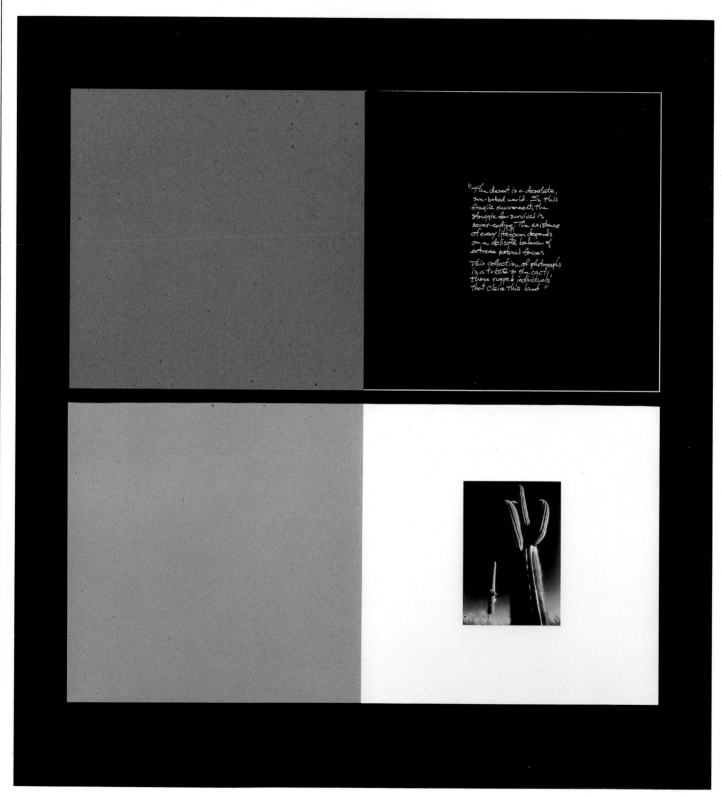

Arthur Meyerson Photography

Photographer Arthur Meyerson's personal trip to Japan resulted in a commemorative brochure that he sent to clients and friends. The four-color brochure of his photographs was made possible because of a trade-out with a design firm and printer. "If it weren't for the trade-out, I probably couldn't have done this. The trade came along at the right moment, so I was able to produce this book."

Audience: *Art directors and designers*
Description: *9" x 9¹/₄" four-color, 32-page brochure*
Quantity: *500*

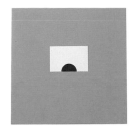

A.M. IN JAPAN

W O O D

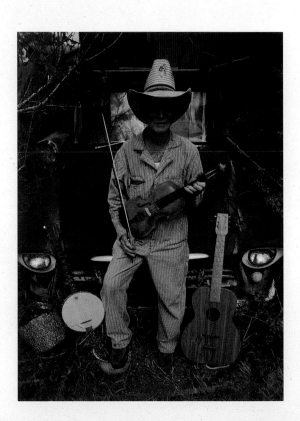

W O R K

Three projects that are based on the principal's names:

Keith Wood Photography

This large-scale poster by Keith Wood is the first of a series of posters playing off the theme "wood." Follow up posters are titled "Wood Wind" and "Wood Boat." Keith supports the image with the copy:

"Keith Wood shoots the back roads of America and the front offices of America's leading corporations. When it comes to photography, Keith Wood works."

Audience: *Art directors and designers*
Description: *16" x 35" full-color poster*
Quantity: *1,500*

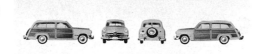

Pirtle Design

The image of the "woody" makes a striking personal letterhead for designer Woody Pirtle. Produced as a personal project, the letterhead appeared quite regularly in design annuals.

Audience: *Corporate and advertising*
Description: *8½" x 11" four-color letterhead*
Quantity: *1,000*

Michael Hart Photography

Photograper Michael Hart sent a T-shirt and card to his clients and prospects with the "Have a Hart" theme as a promotion to tie in with Valentine's Day.

Audience: *Art directors and designers*
Description: *Silkscreened T-shirt and card*
Quantity: *125*

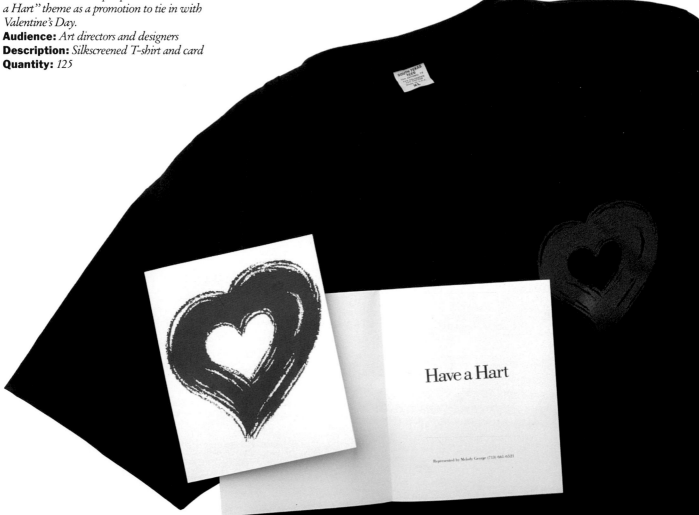

Andy Post Photography
*For photographer Andy Post, the large-scale
mailer to art directors was to make the point
that no project was too big, while at the same
time alluding to the use of large-format
photography. "Andy Post covers every angle of
big production photo shoots. No small job."*
Audience: *Art directors and designers*
Description: *38" x 11½" two-color folder*
Quantity: *1,500*

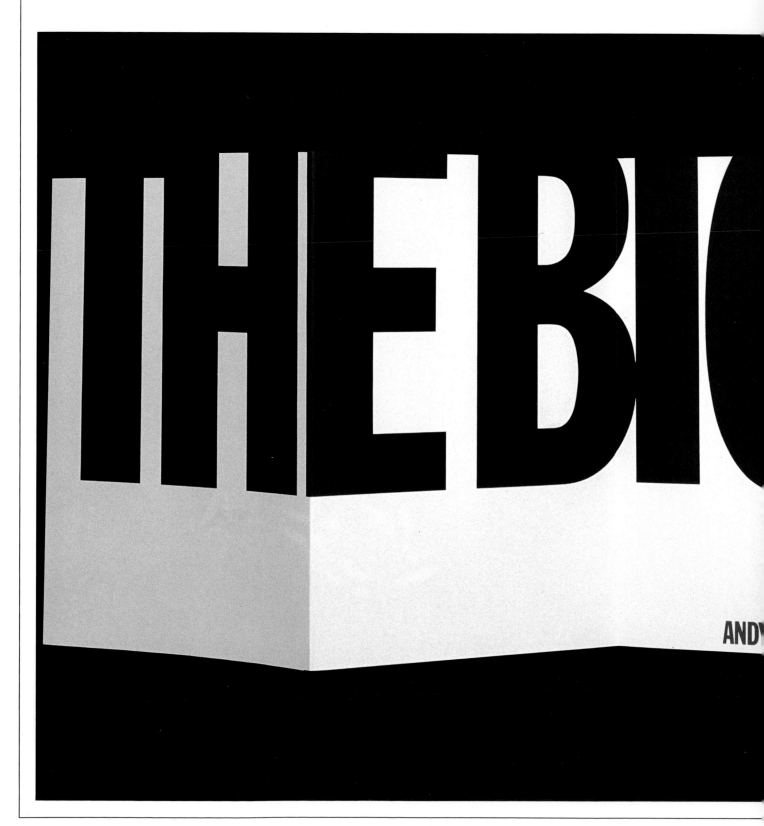

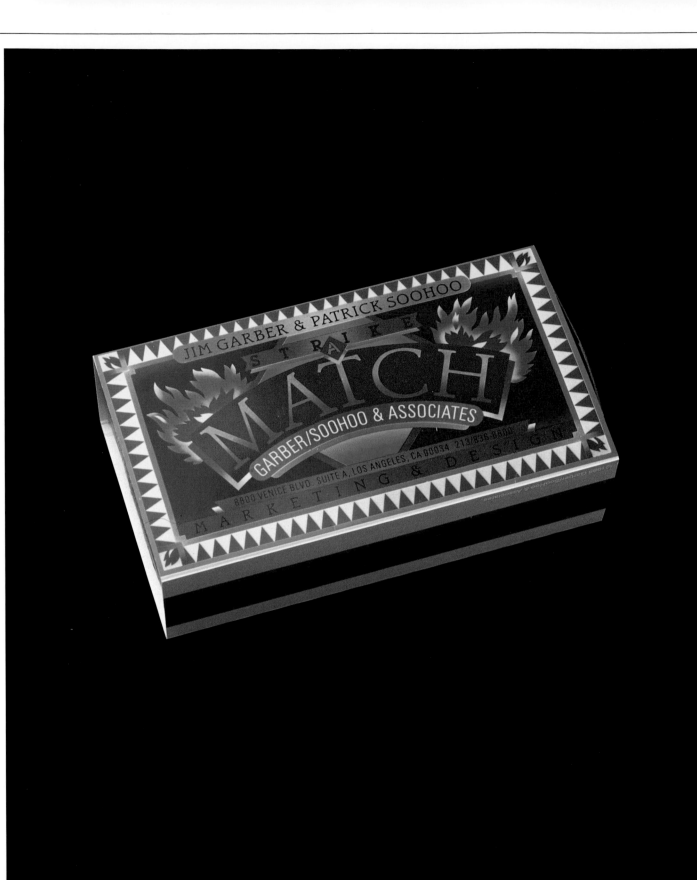

Creative people respond to deadlines. This simple fact may be why so many good promotion items are produced to correspond with changes in addresses or partners, holidays, weddings, births, and anniversaries. The special occasion is seen as a *reason* to communicate, and there is realization with these occasions that if you wait too long, the moment will pass. The "news" won't be new anymore.

Another reason for the high number of very creative solutions for special occasion promotion pieces is that there have already been so many efforts in these areas. When you decide to produce a birth announcement or a Christmas card, you do so well aware that it is not a new vehicle. If you are going to make anyone stop and take notice, you will need to produce the birth announcement or Christmas card with a different slant than has been used before.

The guidelines to use when considering this type of self-promotion are no different from the considerations you should keep in mind for other types of self-promotion. First, ask yourself who the audience is. Who will want to know that you are a proud mother or father? Who will be interested that you have just moved your office? These may be very different audiences.

Second, ask what you can expect from the correspondence. Are you giving out information? Creating good will? Trying to increases business? Win awards? Again, any of these reasons can be acceptable. It is important to know what you expect before you get carried away and spend money without a real plan.

And third, by all means produce the project on time. File cabinets are full of ideas, sketches, and mechanicals for Christmas cards and partnership announcements that were put off and put off until it was too late. (There is one exception where being late has actually helped. For years, Houston designer John Heck has sent out a Christmas card displaying his family's picture in February or March. The response is usually a warm chuckle, knowing how easy it is for all of us to procrastinate.)

For Los Angeles designers Jim Garber and Patrick SooHoo, the need do something timely came when they decided to form a partnership. Playing off the theme "strike a match," the two designers produced a real matchbox (left) and inserted a small brochure (right) that asked prospective clients to call and "fire our imaginations."

Garber/SooHoo & Associates

Facing page: The match box announcement
Below: The 5" x 3" brochure with four-color cover and eight one-color pages that was placed inside the match box, over real matches.
Audience: *Corporate*
Description: *Match box with brochure*
Quantity: *500*

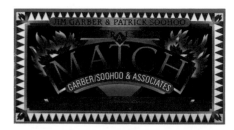

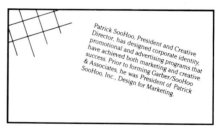

Jim Garber and Patrick SooHoo
are proud to announce
their new partnership.

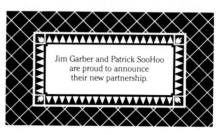

Patrick SooHoo, President and Creative Director, has designed corporate identity, promotional and advertising programs that have achieved both marketing and creative success. Prior to forming Garber/SooHoo & Associates, he was President of Patrick SooHoo, Inc., Design for Marketing.

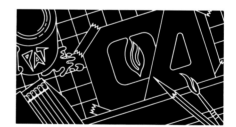

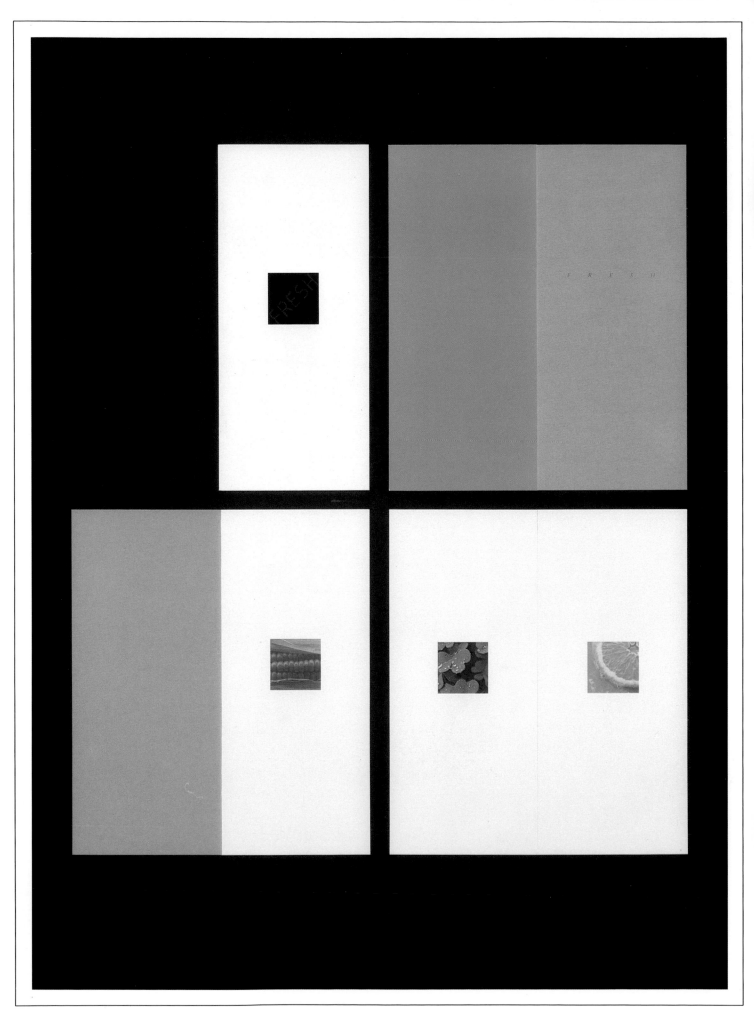

Summerford Design
Jack Summerford announced his new firm with a small brochure titled "Fresh."

"Jack Summerford has made a fresh start."

"After eight years with a prestigious firm, Jack has a fresh office, fresh supplies, fresh coffee and fresh ideas."
Audience: *Corporate*
Description: *3¾" x 8½" four-color, 20-page brochure*
Quantity: *1,000*

Mantel, Koppel & Scher
From the opening page of the brochure, Great Beginnings:

"The longest journey was begun with a single step. In the beginning God created the heaven and earth. Tomorrow is the first day of the rest of your life. Don't put off for tomorrow what you can do today. You have to start somewhere.

"In the spirit of all great beginnings, Richard Mantel, Terry Koppel, and Paula Scher are proud to announce the opening of their new design studio, Mantel, Koppel & Scher.

"The following pages are a celebration of some of the world's great literary beginnings."
Audience: *Corporate and editorial*
Description: *6" x 9" two-color, 28-page brochure*
Quantity: *3,000*

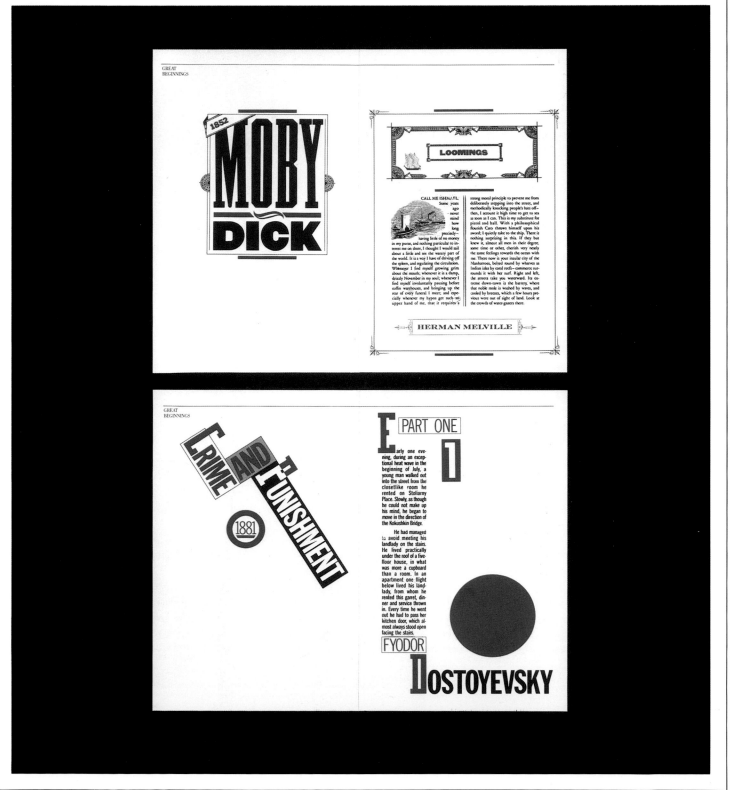

Texas roads symbolized the directions
Mercantile Texas Corporation had
taken and would take. This report
marks my last design job at The
Richards Group. John Stone and Greg
Booth again.

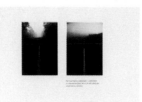

Top: Killeen Mall is located in "the
heart of Texas." Dennard Creative
commissioned this mark for one of
their clients. The neon was just
something I couldn't resist doing.

Bottom: Trademark for Theatre 3,
a Dallas repertory company.

X marked the spot for Expertel,
a telecommunications marketing company. I worked in concert with interior designer Carol Hermanovski on
this project.

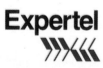

Expertel
>>>|<<<

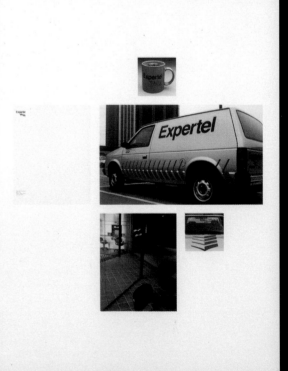

Summerford Design
To celebrate twenty years in the design business, Jack Summerford produced a commemorative book—in a hard-bound and a soft-bound version. The book chronicles his twenty years, illustrated with a project from each year. To assure that he would not send the book out needlessly, Jack mailed a postcard to different lists, and asked for a reply. He found that he sent fewer books with this method, but the follow-up interest was very high.
Audience: *Corporate*
Description: *8½" x 12", 56-page book*
Quantity: *1,500*

Carbone Smolan Associates
To commemorate ten years of their association, Kenneth Carbone and Leslie Smolan published "Ten," a retrospective of work done for 10 clients. Projects were selected to illustrate the diverse scope of services, varying scale of client, and their problem-solving approach to design.
Audience: *Corporate*
Description: *9" x 12" four-color brochure*
Quantity: *2,500*

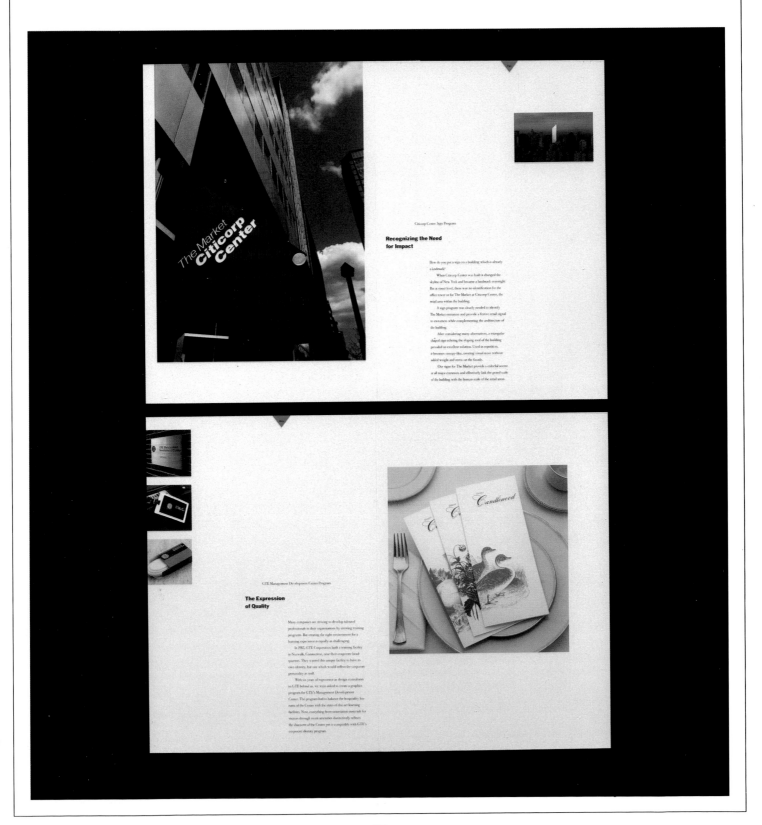

*The mailer announcing the formation of a new
firm with a rather long name used humor to
make a serious statement. By comparing the
name to the names of some of the leading design
firms in the country, Jonson Pirtle Pedersen
Alcorn Metzdorf & Hess was able to say "we
belong in this category of design firms."*
Audience: *Corporate*
Description: *8½" x 11" two-color mailer*
Quantity: *2,000*

ANNOUNCING
THE BIGGEST NAME
IN DESIGN.

ANNOUNCING
THE BIGGEST NAME
IN DESIGN.

Jonson Pirtle Pedersen Alcorn Metzdorf & Hess
45 CHARACTERS

Chermayeff & Geismar Associates
31 CHARACTERS

Anspach Grossman Portugal Inc.
29 CHARACTERS

Pentagram Design Ltd.
20 CHARACTERS

Vignelli Associates
19 CHARACTERS

JONSON PIRTLE PEDERSEN ALCORN METZDORF & HESS, 141 LEXINGTON AVENUE, NEW YORK, NEW YORK 10016 (212) 889-9611

Jerry Haworth Design
Jerry Haworth used the change of address mailer to make the point that his design firm would stay up as late as usual to produce the work. The one-color poster was silkscreened by Jerry in his studio, and the hours were hand-written in with a felt tip pen.
Audience: *Clients and friends*
Description: *8½" x 12" silkscreened mailer*
Quantity: *200*

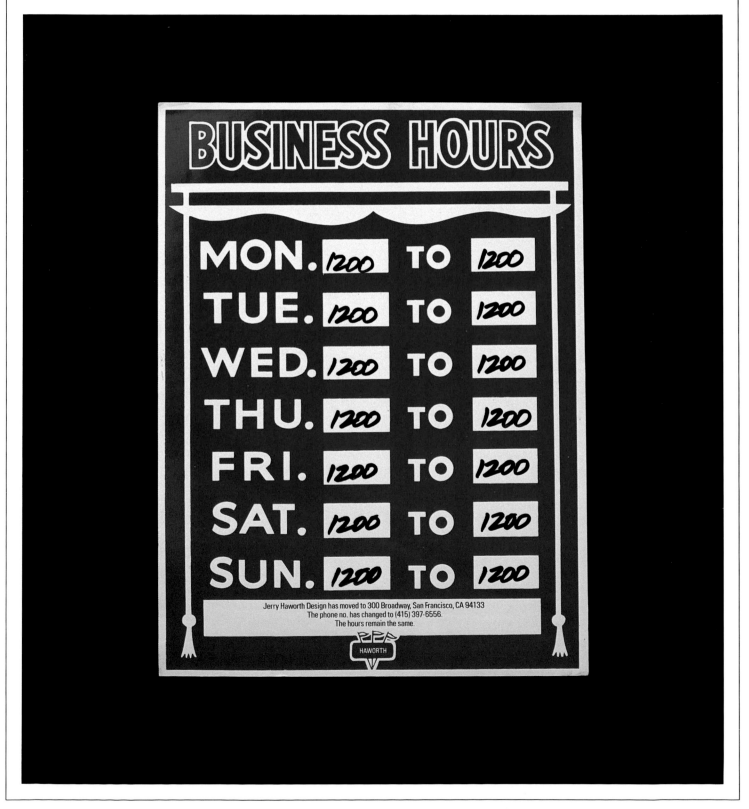

Randall Swatek Associates

Randall Swatek produced a small, simple brochure to celebrate the New Year, and then made sure it was noticed by packaging it in a grand manner. The booklet featured engravings of clocks with sayings about "time," but the real impact was the packaging.

Audience: *Clients and friends*

Description: *4½″ x 4½″ wiro-bound booklet, boxed with colored tissue paper*

Quantity: *400*

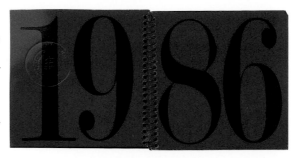

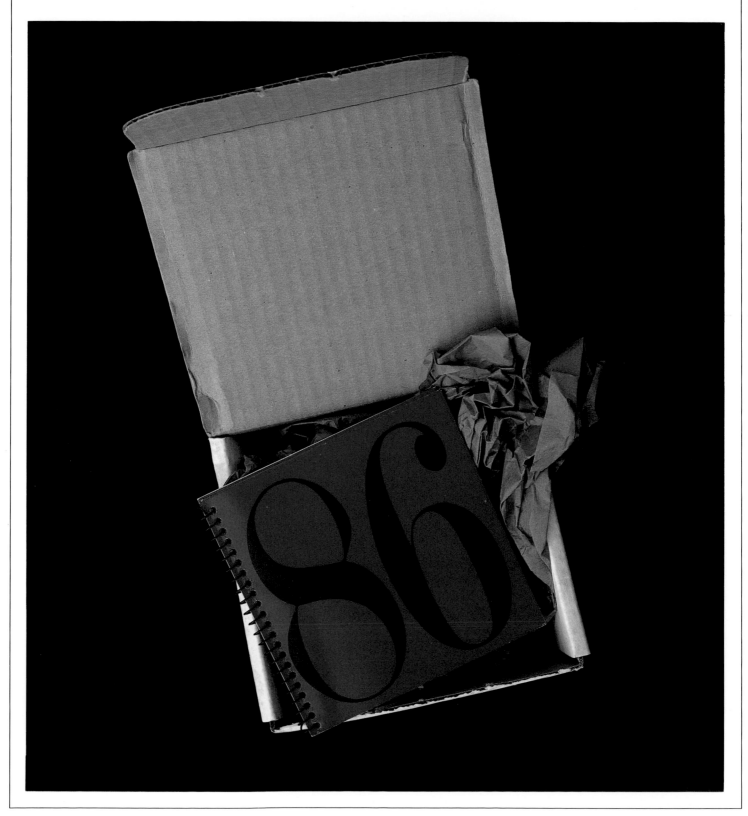

Pannell/St. George

The team of designer Cap Pannell and writer Carol St. George played off their first names to produce a unique image in the crowded world of Christmas cards.
Audience: *Clients and friends*
Description: *17" x 9" four-color card*
Quantity: *500*

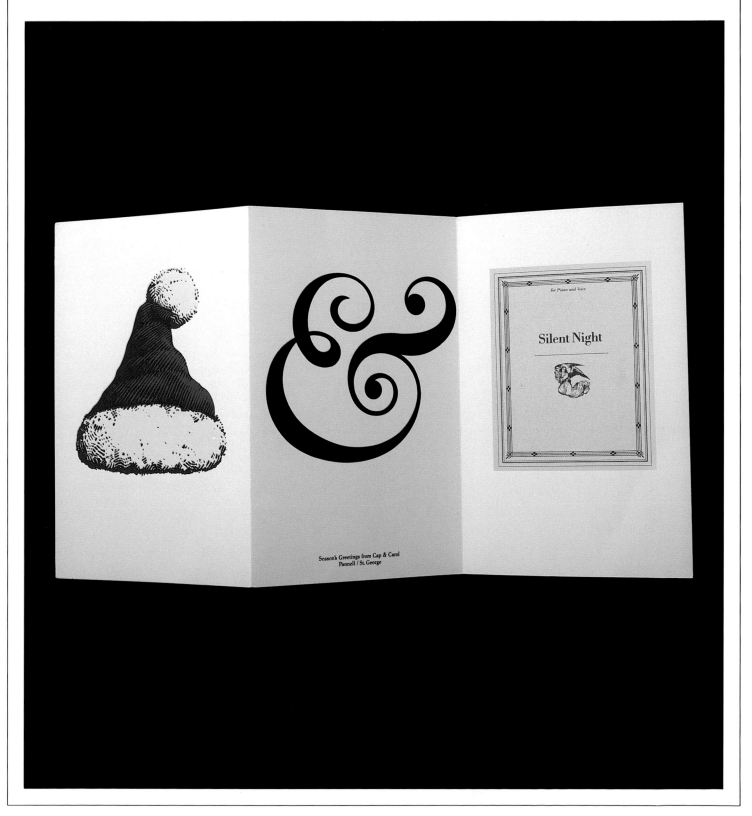

Season's Greetings from Cap & Carol
Pannell / St. George

For Piano and Voice

Silent Night

Chuck & Gayl Carlberg
*The amusing birth announcement of designers
Gayl and Chuck Carlberg was made as a
poster. The rubber baby-bottle nipple was glued
to the two-color poster, and the poster was
rolled into a tube.*
Audience: *Friends*
Description: *24" x 36" two-color poster*
Quantity: *500*

Jonson Pedersen Hinrichs & Shakery
*To announce the move of partner Neil Shakery
to San Francisco from New York, the firm
produced a two-color mailer that folded out to
thirty-six inches. The large photo is printed with
a coarse line pattern on brown craft paper.*
Audience: *Corporate*
Description: *12" x 36" two-color mailer*
Quantity: *750*

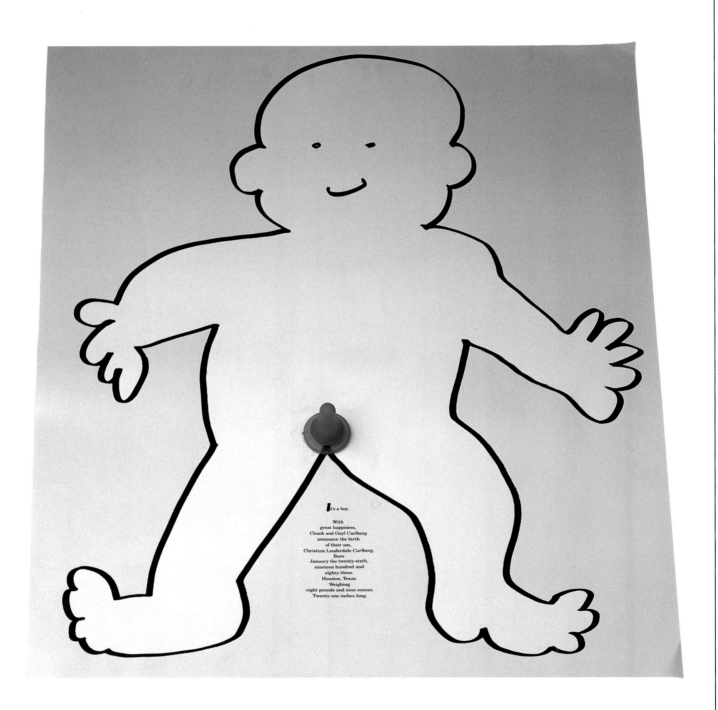

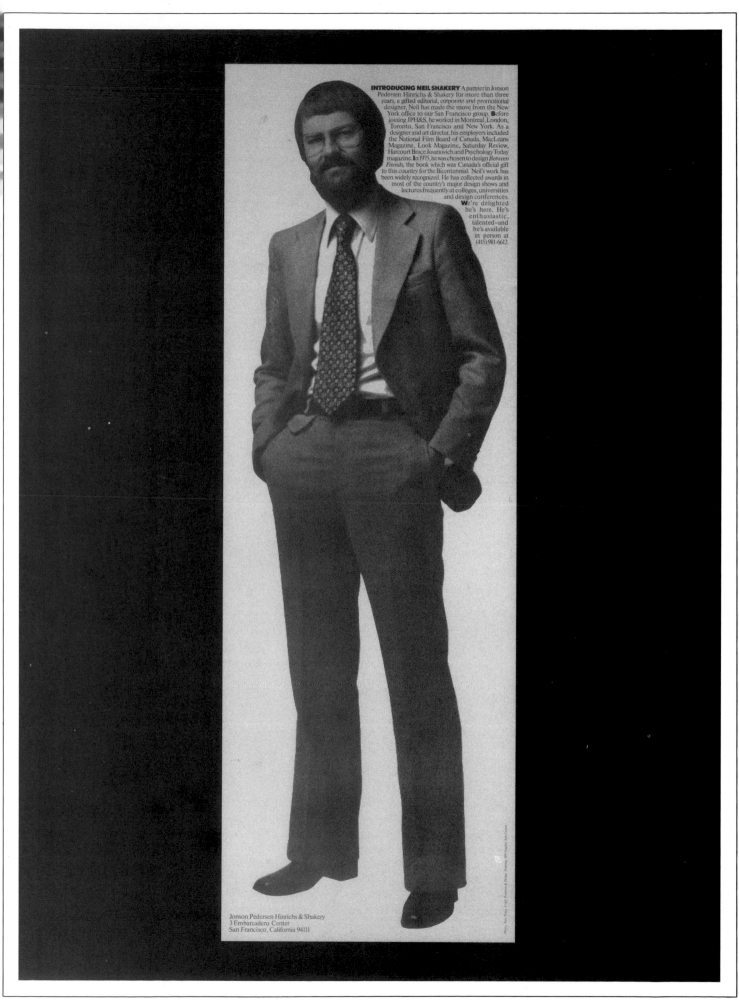

INTRODUCING NEIL SHAKERY A partner in Jonson Pedersen Hinrichs & Shakery for more than three years, a gifted editorial, corporate and promotional designer, Neil has made the move from the New York office to our San Francisco group. Before joining JPH&S, he worked in Montreal, London, Toronto, San Francisco and New York. As a designer and art director, his employers included the National Film Board of Canada, MacLeans Magazine, Look Magazine, Saturday Review, Harcourt Brace Jovanovich and Psychology Today magazine. In 1975, he was chosen to design *Between Friends*, the book which was Canada's official gift to this country for the Bicentennial. Neil's work has been widely recognized. He has collected awards in most of the country's major design shows and lectures frequently at colleges, universities and design conferences. We're delighted he's here. He's enthusiastic, talented–and he's available in person at (415) 981-6612.

Jonson Pedersen Hinrichs & Shakery
3 Embarcadero Center
San Francisco, California 94111

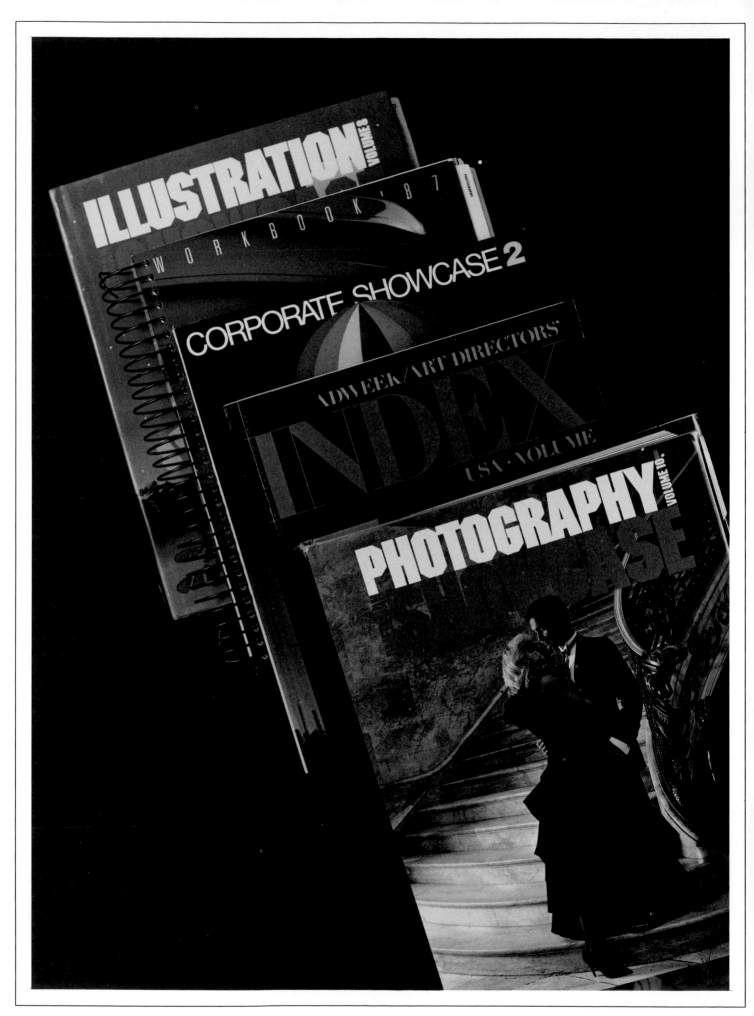

THE DIRECTORIES

Creative directories are one of the better ways for photographers and illustrators, and more recently designers, to reach potential clients. But there is good news and bad news.

The good news is that art buyers—mostly agencies, design firms and in-house marketing staffs—do use the directories to find talent. The directories are excellent sources for new styles and a constant source for talent in other locations. "My ads have paid for themselves," states Houston/New York photographer Steve Brady. "Art directors are able to find a photographer in another location, call him up, negotiate the project and mail a purchase order. It saves trying to figure out from the Yellow Pages who does what." Ads that show local geographic surroundings, or the ability to photograph people (read: corporate officers) seem to draw very well for photographers trying to attract business from other cities. (Table-top or studio photographs, which are readily available in most locations, do not draw as well, we are told.)

For illustrators and designers, style is more important than location. With overnight delivery, illustration and design can now be purchased easily from any part of the country. While it is probably easier to use local talent, most clients will readily go out of town for a unique style.

More good news is the reprints from ads placed in creative directories, which are part of the package price in most cases, are the single largest source for illustrators' and photographers' sample sheets.

The not-so-good news is that the directories are becoming very crowded, and because the page formats are similar, it is harder for your work to stand out. When the name of the game is to make people first notice and then call, the cost of these ads may not be justified for the amount of response.

The best way to determine whether or not you should advertise in the creative directories is to analyze your own situation. Are you at a point where your work, when advertised to a broad audience, will attract enough new business to more than pay for the ads? Should you advertise locally, regionally or nationally? Out of your total budget for promotion, how big a percent would an ad be? Is there anything left to do other sorts of promotions? Do the people that you want to reach use the directories? Which ones? Check around. Ask your peers. What kind of luck have they had? Are they happy with the response? Find out specifically what kind of response they have had. When they say "Good," find out how good. Remember, you are like any other advertiser. You are going to spend real money, and you should know what you are getting for your money.

DIRECTORY TIPS

WHAT SHOULD YOUR AD LOOK LIKE?

- Review the directories and determine which ads you feel work best.
- Keep the ad simple.
- While trying to stand out from the crowd, don't overdesign the ad.
- Keep in mind the ad is to showcase work, not page layout.
- Don't use a lot of small reversed type or distracting backgrounds.
- Keep the number of images on a page to a minimum.

WHICH IMAGES SHOULD BE USED?

- Use only images of the type of work you want. If you want to shoot portraits, resist putting in a sunset, no matter how much you love the shot.
- Use only images that are totally self-explanatory.
- Do not use images that are too abstract, or that will not be effective when reduced to a small size.
- Do not use images that are so subtle that they may suffer in the reproduction.

IS THE AD WORKING?

- Keep track of the calls you receive.
- Keep track of the profit made from directory-influenced work.
- Ask clients if they saw the ad.

ADWEEK PORTFOLIOS

Adweek
49 East 21st Street
New York, NY 10010
(212) 529-5500

Release Date
Spring

Closing Date
September

Full-Page Color Cost
(varies according to distribution)
Agency & Design Firm Package:
Distribution 20,000
Spread, $3,500
Double-Spread, $9,000
Corporate, Annual Report Package:
Distribution 5,000
Spread, $2,000
Double-Spread, $5,100
Publication, Editorial Package:
Distribution 5,000
Spread, $2,000
Double-Spread, $5,100

Combination Buys:
*Agency/Design & Corporate
Annual Report:*
Distribution 25,000
Spread, $4,000
Double-Spread, $10,300
Agency/Design & Publication Editorial:
Distribution 25,000
Spread, $4,000
Double-Spread, $10,300
All Three Distribution Packages:
Distribution 30,000
Spread, $4,500
Double-Spread, $11,600
International Package:
(additional to any of the above)
Full Spread, $500
Double-Spread, $1,500

Full-Page B & W Cost
Same as color.

Production Charges
First color separation free; $150 for each
additional separation

Page Size
17¼ x 10⅞ (spread)

Number Printed
46,000

Free Distribution
30,000 to art directors and art buyers at
ad agencies, design firms and corporations

AMERICAN CORPORATE SHOWCASE

American Showcase
724 Fifth Avenue
New York, NY 10019
(212) 245-0981

Release Date
February

Closing Date
May; final, July

Full-Page Color Cost
By May, $2,100; custom design, $2,800
By July, $2,400; custom design, $3,100

Full-Page B & W Cost
$1,800; custom design, $2,400

Production Charges
Standard pages include typesetting,
mechanical, one separation (to be
retained by printer). Additional color
images are $115; B & W, $75. Custom
designs are full-bleed pages with advertiser's design, type, logo. Advertiser supplies mechanical and camera-ready art.

Page Size
9¼ x 11¾

Number Printed
Minimum projected: 40,000

Free Distribution
U.S. and Canada, 18,000 to only those
hiring visual talent. Names and addresses
pre-verified by phone.

Paid Distribution
23,000; 15,000 in U.S. and Canada;
8,000 internationally.

Reprints
2,000 free on 8 pt. Krome-Kote (light
card) stock.

Other
Standard ads placed alphabetically in
geographic regions. Custom ads placed
in front of each geographic section. Payment plans available. If space reserved
by April, 10% discount.

AMERICAN ILLUSTRATION SHOWCASE

American Showcase
724 Fifth Avenue
New York, NY 10019
(212) 245-0981

Release Date
February

Closing Date
May; final, July

Full-Page Color Cost
By May, $3,000; custom design, $3,600
By July, $3,300; custom design, $3,900

Full-Page B & W Cost
By May, $2,500; custom design, $3,100
By July, $2,800; custom design, $3,400

Production Charges
Standard pages include typesetting,
mechanical, one separation (to be
retained by printer). Additional color
images are $115; B & W, $75. Custom
designs are full-bleed pages with advertiser's design, type, logo. Advertiser supplies mechanical and camera-ready art.

Page Size
9¼ x 11¾

Number Printed
Minimum projected: 40,000

Free Distribution
U.S. and Canada, 18,000 to only those
hiring visual talent. Names and addresses
pre-verified by phone.

Paid Distribution
23,000; 15,000 in U.S. and Canada;
8,000 internationally.

Reprints
2,000 free on 8 pt. Krome-Kote (light
card) stock.

Other
Standard ads placed alphabetically in
geographic regions. Custom ads placed
in front of each geographic section. Payment plans available. If space reserved
by April, 10% discount.

AMERICAN PHOTOGRAPHY SHOWCASE

American Showcase
724 Fifth Avenue
New York, NY 10019
(212) 245-0981

Release Date
February

Closing Date
May; final, July

Full-Page Color Cost
By May, $3,000; custom design, $3,600
By July, $3,300; custom design, $3,900

Full-Page B & W Cost
By May, $2,500; custom design, $3,100
By July, $2,800; custom design, $3,400

Production Charges
Standard pages include typesetting, mechanical, one separation (to be retained by printer). Additional color images are $115; B & W, $75. Custom designs are full-bleed pages with advertiser's design, type, logo. Advertiser supplies mechanical and camera-ready art.

Page Size
9¼ x 11¾

Number Printed
Minimum projected: 40,000

Free Distribution
U.S. and Canada, 18,000 to only those hiring visual talent. Names and addresses pre-verified by phone.

Paid Distribution
23,000; 15,000 in U.S. and Canada; 8,000 internationally.

Reprints
2,000 free on 8 pt. Krome-Kote (light card) stock.

Other
Standard ads placed alphabetically in geographic regions. Custom ads placed in front of each geographic section. Payment plans available. If space reserved by April, 10% discount.

CHICAGO CREATIVE DIRECTORY

333 North Michigan Avenue
Suite 810
Chicago, IL 60601
(312) 236-7337

Release Date
February

Closing Date
November

Full-Page Color Cost
$1,350 (separations provided by photographer)
$2,000 (separations provided by publisher)

Full-Page B & W Cost
$1,000 (photographer supplies mechanical and camera-ready art)

Production Charges
Additional separations, tints, etc. provided at cost.

Page Size
5½ x 8½

Number Printed
10,000

Free Distribution
95% controlled. Total saturation of Chicago market. To top creative directors and art buyers at agencies in 10-state area billing over $1 million; nationally and in Canada to agencies billing over $5 million.

Reprints
1,000 on coated cover stock

THE CREATIVE BLACK BOOK

401 Park Avenue South
New York, NY 10016
(212) 684-4255

Release Date
December

Closing Date
May

Full-Page Color Cost
$6,175

Spread Color Cost
$11,100

Full-Page B & W Cost
$3,990

Spread B & W Cost
$7,260

Production Charges
$130-$180 per image, depending on number of images.

Page Size
6¼ x 10¾

Number Printed
35,500

Free Distribution
19,300 to art directors, art buyers, television producers, copy supervisors, creative group heads at all U.S., Canadian, European ad agencies billing over $5 million.

Paid Distribution
16,000 to corporate ad and promotion people, publications, smaller ad agencies, designers and creative people in 49 countries.

Reprints
2,000 reprints on heavy coated card stock free if mechanicals, art, deposit, production costs and contract in by May. Otherwise, $450 per color page.

Other
Payment plans available. Marketing and creative consultation available.

Prices based on 1987 information.

DESIGNSOURCE	MADISON AVENUE HANDBOOK	THE SILVER BOOK — ASMP
Turnbull & Co. 19 Mount Auburn Street Cambridge, MA 02138 (617) 864-1110	Peter Glenn Publications 17 East 48th Street New York, NY 10017 (212) 688-7940 (800) 223-1254	Annuals Publishing Company 10 East 23rd Street New York, NY 10010 (212) 475-1620

DESIGNSOURCE

Release Date
January

Closing Date
May

Full-Page Color Cost
$1,400

Full-Page B & W Cost
By May 1, $1,200
By May 29, $1,440

Production Charges
First color separation free; $120 each additional. First B & W image free; $50 each additional.

Page Size
5⅛ x 8⅛

Number Printed
10,000

Free Distribution
All decision makers in key ad agencies, design studios, and corporate and publishing in-house art departments in New England.

Reprints
1,000 free

Other
Payment plan available.

MADISON AVENUE HANDBOOK

Release Date
March

Closing Date
November

Full-Page Color Cost
$3,150

Full-Page B & W Cost
$2,150

Production Charges
Each color separation $200 and up.

Page Size
5½ x 8

Number Printed
25,000

Free Distribution
45% controlled distribution to ad agencies, production houses, and corporations. Remainder to mail order, bookstores, others.

Reprints
Color advertisers: 500 on coated card stock with written request 45 days before press. B & W reprints at rate received on request.

Other
10% space discount when advertiser supplies color separations to publisher's specs.

THE SILVER BOOK — ASMP

Release Date
September

Closing Date
February

Full-Page Color Cost
$1,950-$2,150 (depending on deadline met—dates to be set)

Full-Page B & W Cost
$1,950-$2,150 (depending on deadline met—dates to be set)

Production Charges
First color separation free; $100 each additional. First B & W image free; $50 each additional. Photographer to supply finished mechanical.

Page Size
Bleed size 7⅝ x 10½

Number Printed
30,000

Free Distribution
16,000 nationally:
40%—corporate (Fortune 500 companies)
40%—Ad Agencies
20%—editorials (magazines).

Reprints
2,000 on 10 pt. coated card stock

Other
Must be a member of or must join ASMP to place ad. Services include total evaluation of photographer's overall marketing program, portfolio, and suggestions regarding selections for the book.

Prices based on 1987 information.

940 North Highland
Los Angeles, CA 90038
(213) 856-0008

Release Date
January

Closing Date
May; final, May

Full-Page Color Cost
$2,800 (10% discount if paid by June)

Full-Page B & W Cost
$1,850 (10% discount if paid by June)

Production Charges
$100 per color separation; $50 per
halftone

Page Size
8½ x 11

Number Printed
27,000

Free Distribution
15,000 to every major agency, design
studio and in-house art department
across the United States. Every major
agency in cities outside California; 5,600
distributed internationally.

Paid Distribution
6,000 sold in retail markets in U.S.

Reprints
1,000 on coated cover stock

Other
Payment plan available. Corporate list
available to advertisers. Open only
to photographers with studios or reps
in California.

STA 100 SHOW 1985

-TYPOGRAPHY 5 THE ANNUAL OF THE TYPE DIRECTORS CLUB

PRINT XL:IV JULY/AUGUST 1986

PRINT'S REGIONAL DESIGN ANNUAL 1986

graphis annual

graphis posters

6 AIGA GRAPHIC DESIGN USA:6 THE ANNUAL OF THE AMERICAN INSTITUTE OF GRAPHIC ARTS

ILLUSTRATORS 20

AMERICAN ILLUSTRATION 4 BOOTH-CLIBBORN

186 AUGUST 1986 • PHOTOGRAPHY ANNUAL

63rd ART DIRECTORS ANNUAL

HAST

CA

COMPETITIONS AND ANNUALS

One of the more established forms of self-promotion for creative people is the "annual," the time-honored competitive forum for creative work in the advertising, design, illustration, and photography fields. There are annual competitions on the international, national, regional, and local levels. There are competitions for special interests (annual reports, university publications, editorial, etc.), and there are competitions for special disciplines (typography, industrial design, book design, etc.). There are competitions that are "easy" to get work into, and there are others with very difficult odds.

Annual exhibitions have multiplied because they are well accepted. The shows are a stage for new talent, help define current tastes, and are valuable sources for ideas.

Reputations are established through annuals, reputations that influence advancements for employees and attract business for freelancers, firms, and agencies.

With so many exhibitions available, it is important to establish guidelines for entering.

What will be gained from entering the competition? Ego gratification? Peer approval? Show involvement with an organization? New business contacts? All of these reasons are fine. Just be sure that you know when you go into the competition what it is you want to achieve.

Here are our suggestions for entering exhibitions:

—Enter the local awards annual. It is good to be involved with your local club or organization, and the people that will view the awards will *know* who you are, or will after you have won.

—Enter national exhibitions that publish books or catalogs. There are many, so you will have to choose. Which ones are the most prestigious? Which would you want to be in the most? Enter those. It may be one, or it may be four or five or more. Your budget will help determine the number.

—Enter national exhibitions (with books or catalogs) that will be seen by the audience you want to impress. If you are an illustrator, notice which annuals your clients have on their shelves. Chances are these are the ones they are referencing the most.

—Enter exhibitions of special interest to your clients. Designing an annual report? Enter the final book in annual report competitions. If it becomes a winner, you may become a winner with your client. You may only impress one or two people, but these are very important people to you.

COMPETITION GUIDELINES

WHICH SHOWS TO ENTER

- Local competitions
- National exhibitions which publish books or catalogs
- Exhibitions of special interest to your clients

WHAT TO ENTER

- Look in last year's annual and get an idea of what level of work is being accepted in the show. This is only being practical. If there are only 100 accepted entries in a show, it stands to reason that only the *very* best of your work, maybe one or two pieces, has a chance of making the final cut.
- Be critical.
- Don't overenter.

BUDGET

- Establish a budget for entering based on the average number of pieces you will enter on a yearly basis.
- Keep in mind the acceptance or hanging fees.
- Add to your budget the "hidden" costs, such as for delivery or the cost of making prints or slides.

PROMOTE THE RESULTS

- After you have won, make sure your clients are aware of your success.
- For very special awards, send press releases to local business editors.

ADLA ANNUAL

Art Directors' Club of Los Angeles
1258 N. Highland, #209
Los Angeles, California
(213) 465-8707

Affiliation:
Art Directors Club of Los Angeles
(ADLA)

Entry Deadline Month:
July

Average Number of Entries:
4,000

Average Number of Accepted Entries:
400

Single Entry Fee:
$15

Catalog/Book Circulation:
6,000

AMERICAN ILLUSTRATION

American Illustration
67 Irving Place
New York, New York 10003
(212) 460-5558

Entry Deadline Month:
March

Average Number of Entries:
1,200

Average Number of Accepted Entries:
275

Single Entry Fee:
$16

Catalog/Book Circulation:
10,000

ANNUAL OF AMERICAN ILLUSTRATION

Society of Illustrators
128 East 63rd St.
New York, New York 10021
(212) 838-2560

Affiliation:
Society of Illustrators

Entry Deadline Month:
October

Average Number of Entries:
2,000

Average Number of Accepted Entries:
650

Single Entry Fee:
$15

Catalog/Book Circulation:
10,000

ART DIRECTORS' ANNUAL

Art Directors' Club
250 Park Avenue South
New York, New York 10003
(212) 674-0500

Affiliation:
Art Directors' Club of New York

Entry Deadline Month:
May

Average Number of Entries:
16,500

Average Number of Accepted Entries:
1,750

Single Entry Fee:
$20 (Print)

Catalog/Book Circulation:
20,000

AMERICAN PHOTOGRAPHY

American Photography
67 Irving Place
New York, New York 10003
(212) 460-5558

Entry Deadline Month:
November

Average Number of Entries:
1,000

Average Number of Accepted Entries:
200

Single Entry Fee:
$16

Catalog/Book Circulation:
10,000

CA ADVERTISING ANNUAL

Communication Arts
410 Sherman Avenue
P.O. Box 10300
Palo Alto, California 94303
(415) 326-6040

Affiliation:
Communication Arts Magazine

Entry Deadline Month:
July

Average Number of Entries:
10,000

Average Number of Accepted Entries:
300

Single Entry Fee:
$15

Catalog/Book Circulation:
60,000

Prices based on 1987 information.

CA DESIGN ANNUAL

Communication Arts
410 Sherman Avenue
P.O. Box 10300
Palo Alto, California 94303
(415) 326-6040

Affiliation:
Communication Arts Magazine

Entry Deadline Month:
July

Average Number of Entries:
14,000

Average Number of Accepted Entries:
225

Single Entry Fee:
$15

Catalog/Book Circulation:
60,000

CA PHOTOGRAPHY ANNUAL

Communication Arts
410 Sherman Avenuc
P.O. Box 10300
Palo Alto, California 94303
(415) 326-6040

Affiliation:
Communication Arts Magazine

Entry Deadline Month:
March

Average Number of Entries:
5,500

Average Number of Accepted Entries:
150

Single Entry Fee:
$12

Catalog/Book Circulation:
60,000

CREATIVITY

Creativity
10 East 39th St.
New York, New York 10016
(212) 889-6500

Affiliation:
Art Direction Magazine

Entry Deadline Month:
May

Average Number of Entries:
11,000

Average Number of Accepted Entries:
1,200

Single Entry Fee:
$9.50

Catalog/Book Circulation:
10,000

CA ILLUSTRATION ANNUAL

Communication Arts
410 Sherman Avenue
P.O. Box 10300
Palo Alto, California 94303
(415) 326-6040

Affiliation:
Communication Arts Magazine

Entry Deadline Month:
March

Average Number of Entries:
5,500

Average Number of Accepted Entries:
190

Single Entry Fee:
$12

Catalog/Book Circulation:
60,000

COMMUNICATION GRAPHICS

AIGA
1059 Third Avenue
New York, New York 10021
(212) 752-0813

Affiliation:
American Institute of Graphic Arts
(AIGA)

Entry Deadline Month:
February

Average Number of Entries:
5,000

Average Number of Accepted Entries:
125

Single Entry Fee:
$18 ($10 Member)

Catalog/Book Circulation:
12,000

DESI AWARDS

Desi Graphics Awards
32 Gansevoort
New York, New York 10014
(212) 741-7331

Affiliation:
Graphic Design: USA

Entry Deadline Month:
January

Average Number of Entries:
4,500

Average Number of Accepted Entries:
650-700

Single Entry Fee:
$12.00

Catalog/Book Circulation:
2,000

THE BOOK SHOW

AIGA
1059 Third Avenue
New York, New York 10021
(212) 752-0813

Affiliation:
American Institute of Graphic Arts
(AIGA)

Entry Deadline Month:
December

Average Number of Entries:
750

Average Number of Accepted Entries:
100

Single Entry Fee:
$18 ($10 Member)

Catalog/Book Circulation:
12,000

THE ONE SHOW

The One Club
3 West 18th St.
New York, New York 10011
(212) 255-7070

Affiliation:
The One Club

Entry Deadline Month:
June

Average Number of Entries:
12,000

Average Number of Accepted Entries:
500

Single Entry Fee:
$45 (Print)

Catalog/Book Circulation:
8,500

PHOTOGRAPHIS ANNUAL

Graphis Press Corp.
107 Dufourstrasse
CH-8008 Zurich
Switzerland

Affiliation:
Graphis Magazine

Entry Deadline Month:
June

Average Number of Entries:
3,500

Average Number of Accepted Entries:
500

Single Entry Fee:
$10

Catalog/Book Circulation:
9,000

MEAD ANNUAL REPORT SHOW

Mead Paper
Fine Paper Division
Courthouse Plaza Northeast
Dayton, Ohio 45463
(513) 222-6323

Affiliation:
Mead Paper

Entry Deadline Month:
May

Average Number of Entries:
750

Average Number of Accepted Entries:
35

Single Entry Fee:
$20

Catalog/Book Circulation:
1,500

PHOTO/DESIGN

Photo/Design
One Park Avenue
New York, New York 10016
(212) 000-0000

Affiliation:
Photo/Design Magazine

Entry Deadline Month:
September

Average Number of Entries:
3,000

Average Number of Accepted Entries:
100

Single Entry Fee:
$10

Catalog/Book Circulation:
30,000

PRINT'S CASEBOOKS

Best in Advertising
Best in Covers & Posters
Best in Annual Reports
Best in Packaging
Best in Exhibition Design
Best in Environmental Graphics

Print Magazine
104 Fifth Avenue, 9th Floor
New York, New York 10011
(212) 463-0600

Affiliation:
Print Magazine

Entry Deadline Month:
June

Average Number of Entries:
20,000

Average Number of Accepted Entries:
250

Single Entry Fee:
$10 to $25

Catalog/Book Circulation:
7,500

Prices based on 1987 information.

PRINT'S REGIONAL DESIGN ANNUAL

Print Magazine
104 Fifth Avenue, 9th Floor
New York, New York 10011
(212) 463-0600

Affiliation:
Print Magazine

Entry Deadline Month:
March

Average Number of Entries:
38,000

Average Number of Accepted Entries:
1,600

Single Entry Fee:
$12.50

Catalog/Book Circulation:
62,000

STA 100

STA
233 E. Ontario St.
Suite 301
Chicago, Illinois 60611
(312) 787-2018

Affiliation:
Society of Typographic Arts (STA)

Entry Deadline Month:
May

Average Number of Entries:
2,000

Average Number of Accepted Entries:
100

Single Entry Fee:
$25 ($20 Member)

Catalog/Book Circulation:
3,000

GRAPHIS BI-ANNUALS

GRAPHIS ANNUAL REPORTS

GRAPHIS PACKAGING

Graphis Press Corp.
107 Dufourstrasse
CH-8008 Zurich
Switzerland

Affiliation:
Graphis Magazine

Single Entry Fee:
$10

Catalog/Book Circulation:
7,500

GRAPHIS ANNUAL

Graphis Press Corp.
107 Dufourstrasse
CH-8008 Zurich
Switzerland

Affiliation:
Graphis Magazine

Entry Deadline Month:
January

Average Number of Entries:
5,000

Average Number of Accepted Entries:
500

Single Entry Fee:
$10

Catalog/Book Circulation:
12,000

TYPOGRAPHY

Type Directors Club
545 West 45th Street
New York, New York 10036
(212) 983-6042

Affiliation:
Type Directors Club

Entry Deadline Month:
January

Average Number of Entries:
3,500

Average Number of Accepted Entries:
200

Single Entry Fee:
$10

Catalog/Book Circulation:
10,000

GRAPHIS POSTER ANNUAL

Graphis Press Corp.
107 Dufourstrasse
CH-8008 Zurich
Switzerland

Affiliation:
Graphis Magazine

Entry Deadline Month:
June

Average Number of Accepted Entries:
475

Single Entry Fee:
$10

Catalog/Book Circulation:
7,000

ADVERTISING PHOTOGRAPHERS OF AMERICA	ART DIRECTORS CLUB OF NEW YORK	SOCIETY OF ILLUSTRATORS

Advertising Photographers of America
45 East 20th Street
New York, New York 10003
(212) 254-5500

Membership:
Primarily commercial photographers

Members:
2,000

Chapters:
Five Chapters

Benefits:
Bi-monthly newsletter, four meetings per year, discounts on seminars, health plan

Cost:
$300 full membership
$150 associate membership
$75 assistant membership

Art Directors Club of New York
250 Park Avenue
New York, New York 10003
(212) 674-0500

Membership:
Primarily art directors, designers, writers

Members:
800

Chapters:
No

Benefits:
Annual exhibitions, presentations and dinners Hall of Fame

Cost:
$185 full membership (In New York)
Out-of-town membership fees vary

Society of Illustrators
128 East 63rd Street
New York, New York 10021
(212) 838-2560

Membership:
Primarily professional illustrators

Members:
1,000

Chapters:
No

Benefits:
Members only club, gallery, exhibits, annual competition, annual book

Cost:
$275 full membership (New York)
$125 full membership (Outside New York)

AIGA	ASMP	STA

American Institute of Graphic Arts
1059 Third Avenue
New York, New York 10021
(212) 752-0813

Membership:
Primarily graphic designers

Members:
5,000

Chapters:
Seventeen chapters

Benefits:
Bi-monthly journal, publications, national directory, annual exhibits, annual book, group health plan, bi-annual national conference

Cost:
$125 full membership
Additional for chapter membership

The American Society
of Magazine Photographers
205 Lexington Avenue
New York, New York 10016
(212) 889-9144

Membership:
Primarily professional photographers

Members:
5,100

Chapters:
Thirty-three chapters

Benefits:
Monthly meetings, series of publications, studio insurance

Cost:
$225 general membership
$125 associate membership
$75 assistant membership
$50 student membership

Society of Typographic Arts
233 East Ontario Street
Chicago, Illinois 60611
(312) 787-2018

Membership:
Primarily graphic designers

Members:
2,000

Chapters:
No

Benefits:
Workshops, seminars, publications, annual conference, design journal, annual exhibition, annual book

Cost:
$80 full membership (Chicago)
$50 full membership (Outside Chicago)

Prices based on 1987 information.

ORGANIZATIONS

No matter what you do, there is probably an organization of people that do the same thing. Organizations are the networks that creative people use to gain insight into their businesses, find new job opportunities, or find client contacts. Reasons for organization membership range from practical business considerations to fullfilling the need to belong, to make contact and share ideas with people that share your interests. And they are good social environments, as well.

It is important to join the organizations that best fit your needs. On the facing page is a list of six national organizations that cater to the interests of creative people in the art direction, graphic design, writing, photography and illustration areas. Many other national groups exist with more specialized interests, such as the Society of Publication Designers or the Type Directors Club. Membership in smaller, more focused clubs generally is helpful for the professional that is not having his or her needs met by a larger organization. Many times these same professionals will belong to multiple organizations.

It is also important to be a member of the local clubs as well as the national organizations. Most metropolitan areas offer a range of local clubs, the art directors club being the most popular. The local art directors club generally is made up of art directors, designers, photographers, illustrators, writers, and a range of suppliers from typesetters and retouchers to printers and paper merchants. The mix of disciplines that make up the local organizations lead to many business and social contacts. It is in these organizations that many professionals get their first chance at helping to organize and manage large projects, such as competitions and seminars.

Most metropolitan areas also have a chapter of the national advertising or public relations organizations, such as the American Association of Advertising Agencies, Inc. (AAAA), Public Relations Society of America (PRSA), or the International Association of Business Communicators (IABC). Membership in local chapters of national organizations offers the best of both worlds, local meetings on the one hand and national competitions and conventions and the other. National organizations such as AIGA and ASMP have local chapters in some areas but not in others.

INDEX